Getting Ready to Start School

By Netmums and available from Headline

Baby Sleep Solutions
Baby's First Year
Feeding Kids
Getting Ready to Start School
How to Be a Happy Mum
Toddling to Ten
Your Pregnancy

Helen Stoker

Getting Ready to Start School

parents and experts share advice and experience

with Hilary Pereira and Hollie Smith

headline

First published in 2010
by HEADLINE PUBLISHING GROUP

1

The purpose of this book is offer advice based on the experience of other parents. The author and publisher cannot take responsibility for any person acting as a result of the information contained in this book. Parents are advised to refer to the websites listed on pages 195–8 in order to have information that is up to date and relevant to the location in which they live.

Cataloguing in Publication Data is available from the British Library

Trade paperback ISBN 978 0 7553 6102 1

Typeset in Clearface Regular by Palimpsest Book Production Limited, Falkirk, Stirlingshire

Printed and bound in Great Britain by Clays Ltd, St Ives plc

Headline's policy is to use papers that are natural, renewable and recyclable products and made from wood grown in sustainable forests. The logging and manufacturing processes are expected to conform to the environmental regulations of the country of origin.

HEADLINE PUBLISHING GROUP
An Hachette UK Company
338 Euston Road
London NW1 3BH

www.headline.co.uk
www.hachette.co.uk

Contents

Author's note

Broadly speaking, much of the information in this book is relevant across the UK. However, for simplicity's sake, it focuses on England and, because of differences in the way education systems work within the UK, there may be information here that does not apply if you live in Wales, Northern Ireland or Scotland. All the links you need to find out about education in these areas are included in the back of the book.

Introduction

Can you believe your little one is getting ready to start school? It seems only yesterday that they were helpless, cuddly little babies; then adorable, infuriating, gorgeous toddlers. During this time you have helped them learn how to walk and run, to eat with a knife and fork, go to the toilet, dress, wash (sometimes, anyway) and to be entertaining little companions capable of holding proper, interesting conversations. But are they ready – and are you ready – for the world of Big School?

Starting school truly is the next big phase in your child's life and, of course, you want to do everything you can to make the transition as smooth as possible. There are lots of new issues to face, many of which can be confusing, worrying, and even a bit scary, especially if it's your first child putting that uniform on for the first time.

There are the practical issues: just how do you know what is the best school for your child? How does the application system work? How early should you be looking into all this? Then, almost as soon as you get that letter confirming your school place, a whole new set of worries creep in: what if they aren't ready? What if they don't like it? What if they don't make any friends? Will anyone notice if they get left out or left behind? Who will make sure they eat their lunch?

And then there's you. At Netmums, we understand that it's often the mums who are most worried about making new friends and fitting in at the school gate, not the children! How do *you* feel about your baby starting school? What does this mean for your life now?

That's why I am so pleased to bring you this book, which leads you through all the issues, practical and emotional. Our expert team – led by Netmums' author Hilary – gives you all the behind-the-scenes information you need about how schools operate, what your child will experience and how to give your child the best possible preparation in advance. And, of course, as always with Netmums, there are the invaluable experiences of many mums who have guided their children through the process and seen them settle happily into school life. This is your chance to take advantage of the collective wisdom of many mums who have trodden the new-school path before you and lived to tell the tale.

Thinking about my first child starting school brings to mind the phrase, 'The hardest part of having children is letting them go.' For me, starting school was the first stage in the process of letting my children go – letting them grow up to become their own little person where I'm not always around to soothe, supervise and kiss scratched knees. But the best bit is collecting them at 3pm: seeing them run happily out of those gates and into my arms, waving and yelling goodbye to their friends, and arriving full of chat about what they've done that day. It's then that you realise, you don't know why you were worried.

Siobhan Freegard
Founder, Netmums

Meet the team

Hilary Pereira is a journalist and author with a special interest in parenting. Among other titles, she is author of *Your Pregnancy* for Netmums. A former deputy editor of *Mother & Baby* magazine, she writes for a wide range of media, including magazines and websites, and has appeared on news programmes representing the view of Netmums' members. She is also a mum with recent experience of school selection and all that goes along with it. Hilary is married and lives in south London.

Hollie Smith is a journalist and parenting author who has written seven books, including three other titles for Netmums: *Baby Sleep Solutions*, *Toddling to Ten*, and *Baby's First Year*. A member of Netmums for the past eight years, she is a firm believer in the importance of friendship, support and solidarity among mums. Hollie lives in Bedfordshire with her husband and two daughters, aged eight and six.

Emma Hall qualified as a teacher from the University of Plymouth in 1996 with a BEd (Hons) in Primary Education and began her career as a Year 6 teacher in a Hampshire primary school. She then moved to a large primary in Hillingdon, where she became deputy head in 2002. A trustee at her local pre-school, she is currently taking a break from teaching to be at home with her two young children, the eldest of whom recently started primary school.

Dr Bob Burden is Emeritus Professor of Applied Educational Psychology at the University of Exeter. Before joining the university in 1971 to establish its first training course for educational psychologists, he worked both as a teacher and educational psychologist. He is a Past President of the International School Psychology Association, from which he has received a lifetime achievement award for his contribution to international school psychology. He is the author of several books and over 100 published articles and book chapters on the application of psychological principles and research to supporting children's development in school. Bob is the father of three sons and has five granddaughters.

1 Pre-school days

Why learning starts early

Your little one takes her first steps towards full-time education way before that red-letter day when she actually starts at 'big school'. In many ways, the two years beforehand offer a vital training run for school life and, in particular, the chance to get a head start on the all-important process of learning through play.

Of course, much of her preparation for school takes place at home, with you. But if you send your child to a care provider such as a nursery, playgroup or pre-school, it will encourage her to mix with other children – an ability she's going to need in abundance when she starts school for real. And it will help her to find her feet without you around, which is likely to make the separation at the school gates, when the time comes, a good deal easier. (For both of you!)

More specifically, she'll have more chance of acquiring some vital skills, including hand-eye co-ordination, co-operation and teamwork, listening and following instructions. In fact, children who attend some form of early learning setting are thought to be gaining more benefit than ever before when it comes to their development, and studies have backed this – so it's official! For example, the Effective Provision of Pre-School Education (EPPE) Project – which looked at the development of children between the ages of three and seven, and compared those who'd attended a range of providers, including private and local authority nurseries, playgroups and pre-schools, with those who had limited or no pre-school experience – found that, overall, pre-school experience *enhanced* development and that 'high-quality' pre-schooling boosted a child's intellectual, social and behavioural development still further. The project also found that starting pre-schooling early (under the age of three) was related to better intellectual development and that disadvantaged children, in particular, stand to benefit.

What the Netmums say

The benefits of pre-school settings

I was on maternity leave with my second child when my eldest, Sophia, started nursery school and it was great for her as it developed her social skills with other young children. Also, since the nursery school was attached to the primary school it made transition from nursery to the Reception year a lot easier, as she was already comfortable with the school environment, the playground, the familiar faces of the teacher and generally the school facilities. She felt a lot calmer and happy to start 'big school'. It had a positive effect on Mia, too, indirectly. It was a lot easier for her when she went to nursery, knowing well in advance how it was going to be because of seeing her older sister going.

Claudia from Bedford, mum to Sophia, nine, and Mia, seven

Pre-school was great for both me and my son. We were lucky enough to know several other children starting at around the same time from toddler groups. It was small and run by excellent staff. Will never had anxious moments. And it definitely made starting school easier as they had already been introduced to forms of learning and he was ready for the challenge of school (despite being a summer baby and only just four when he started). On a more personal note, the staff helped me support Will through the difficult time when his dad and I separated. They were happy to speak privately to me and keep an extra eye on him, which was invaluable.
Jane from Hull, mum to Will, nine

Both my girls gained a huge amount through their playgroups and nursery places. One of the most important things was social skills – learning to make friends but also to be in a large group of different children and coping with the hustle and bustle of this. Another huge thing was getting used to a routine within a large group. Although there was a lot of free play they also got used to the simple routines of hanging their coats up, sitting on the carpet at certain times, lining up to go out to play, organising things for snack time, etc, all of which helped them get used to the much stricter routines of the school day. It was also a great way for them to gain confidence, to learn to stand on their own two feet in the big world without Mummy, and to learn how to trust the grown-ups and ask for help when they needed it. Finally, the practical skills they gained were invaluable – simple things like putting on their own shoes, hanging up their own coats, finding their own plates for a snack and being able to go to the toilet on their own. Of course, they both learnt a lot through play and the Early Years Foundation Stage curriculum, too, which aided their readiness for school.
Nicola from Edinburgh, mum to Hannah, eight, and Feena, six

The Early Years Foundation Stage

All registered pre-schooling providers must follow a structure of education and care that forms a part of the National Curriculum (see page 18) and is called the Early Years Foundation Stage (EYFS). The activities on offer to children in registered pre-school settings are all carefully designed to fulfil its requirements, which cover six key areas: personal, social and emotional development; communication, language and literacy; problem solving, reasoning and numeracy; knowledge and understanding of the world; physical development; and creative development.

If you think some of that sounds rather serious for children as young as three, bear in mind that it's all based upon the principle of learning through play – for example, building a LEGO tower or crawling through a tunnel to boost physical development; model making or drawing for creative development; water and sand play or bug hunts for knowledge and understanding of the world; and role play or dressing up for personal, social and emotional development.

Also central to the EYFS is an emphasis on helping children to develop on an individual basis and the need for progress to be assessed through observations which are carefully recorded so parents can be kept informed.

To make sure settings are abiding by this framework, they must be inspected and approved by Ofsted – the Office for Standards in Education, Children's Services and Skills (for more on Ofsted and its equivalents in Wales, Scotland and Northern Ireland, see page 20).

The EYFS continues to be relevant once your child starts school. There's more about it in Chapters 5 and 6.

Free early learning entitlements

Thanks to the early years funding that's on offer from the Government, all three- and four-year-olds in England and Wales are entitled to 15 hours of free part-time early learning or day care provision per week, for 38 weeks of the year. (Similar entitlements are available in Scotland and Northern Ireland: sources of further information about these are included in Appendix III at the back of the book.) Precisely when your child becomes eligible for this funding depends on when she was born: those with a birthday between 1 January and 31 March become eligible on 1 April following their third birthday; those with a birthday between 1 April and 31 August become eligible on 1 September following their third birthday; and those with a birthday between 1 September and 31 December become eligible on 1 January following their third birthday.

Until very recently, these free hours had to be taken in equal chunks over five days. But changes to the rules mean there's now a bit more flexibility and – depending on what's on offer in terms of days and hours at the provider in question – they can be spread across three days, making longer sessions a possibility. Of course, some providers may only be open for short sessions or on certain days anyway – do check before making any plans.

Your free hours can be taken up at a range of different providers, as long as they are Ofsted inspected and have registered to take part, and that includes state-run and private nurseries, pre-schools, playgroups and accredited childminders. (If it suits you to do so, you can spread the funding across two different providers.)

Bear in mind that many popular settings fill up quickly – in some cases you can't automatically expect a place and may have to go on a waiting list. If you haven't already, it's worth thinking ahead and making plans well before your child turns three.

There's more information about all of these choices in the box on page 6 – and you can find out more about providers in your area, and which providers offer free places, by contacting your local authority's Family Information Service (also sometimes known as Children's Information Service). There is a national number and website, which will help you pinpoint the right contact details for your area – details are in Appendix III at the back of the book.

You don't have to do anything to claim the funding, but you'll be asked by staff at your provider to sign what's called a parent declaration form, so they can fill in the paperwork and make the claim on your behalf.

Extra help

If early learning funding doesn't cover the full cost of your childcare needs, you may be able to get some further help, either from Working Tax Credits or employer-supported childcare, which includes the childcare voucher scheme. Students, lone parents and those returning to work after unemployment may also be able to get some help from the government with childcare costs.

There's further information at Direct Gov or from the Daycare Trust's Paying for Childcare site. Details for these – and all the other useful sources of information and help mentioned elsewhere – are listed in the appendix at the back of the book.

Your childcare and early learning options

Private nursery

Private nurseries, sometimes known as day nurseries, are run on a commercial basis by individuals or companies. They are usually open all day, typically from early morning to early evening, and fees, which vary greatly, are on average £167 a week, although they can be as much as £400. Staff ratios, legally required by Ofsted, are one adult to three children under two years; one adult to four children aged two years; and one adult to eight children aged three to seven years.

If you work, your little one may already be a regular

attendee at a private nursery by the time she becomes eligible for her free early learning place at three, and it may suit you – perhaps because of work commitments, or because you know she's well settled – to keep her there. The good news is that some private nurseries are registered with the early learning funding scheme, allowing parents to take up their 15 free hours, while paying for any 'top-up' hours they need beyond them. Your nursery should automatically let you know if it's an option, apply for the funding on your behalf, and make the appropriate reduction from your fees for you.

Not all private nurseries are registered and able to offer a funded place, though – you'll need to check first.

State-run nursery

Nursery schools and classes run by the local authority may be attached to a primary school, a children's centre, or operate independently. Intended to be a gentle stepping stone to school life for three- and four-year-olds, they're staffed by qualified nursery teachers and assistants or nursery nurses and tend to offer more structured learning than pre-schools or playgroups (see page 8). Staff ratios are two adults to 20 to 26 children, with one of the adults required to be a qualified teacher, the other a qualified nursery assistant.

At state-run nurseries there are no fees to pay – although you may be asked to pay for snacks and meals, make other donations, or even to take part in fundraising activities. Typically they only offer funded places during school hours and term times, although some also offer extended hours for which they charge a 'top-up' fee.

Nursery classes and schools have an admissions system just like primary schools and you need to apply for a place in advance of your child's third birthday. Contact the teacher in charge to find out if there's a space available – if there is, you'll be asked to fill out an application form. Many state-run nurseries are oversubscribed, so bear this in mind to avoid disappointment.

If there's a nursery attached to the primary school you hope your child will later attend (it may be in the school building itself, or in a separate unit nearby), it makes sense to try and get your little one a place there. It will offer a great chance for her to become familiar with the surroundings and she's bound to make friends who will move with her at the same time. A word of warning, though: don't assume that getting at place for your child in a nursery will guarantee her a place later on at the attached school. You will still need to apply for a school place when the time comes (there's more on this on page 55) and there may not be enough places for all who would like one, whether or not they already attend the nursery.

Pre-school/playgroup

Pre-schools or playgroups typically take children aged from two and a half to three and up, and tend to operate short, informal sessions of either a morning or afternoon, with the aim of easing a child gently into a sociable learning environment. At least half the staff must be formally trained and most look to parents for some voluntary help, too. Ratios are one adult to four children for children under two, and one adult to eight children for children aged three to five years.

Session fees are on average £4 to £7, but most are happy to offer funded places, which you can take advantage of once your child is eligible.

Childminder

Childminders are self-employed and provide childcare in their own home, charging fees of between £2.50 to £7.50 an hour. They can register for up to six children under eight years, including no more than one under 12 months, and they must take their own children into account.

It's quite possible to claim your early years funding through a childminder, but only if she's registered with Ofsted and is a member of a National Childminding Association Children Come First accredited network. If she isn't, you might choose to combine her services and a funded pre-school or local authority nursery by asking her to drop off and collect your little one from a suitable setting where free places are available. And you might want to make a switch to that same combination if you work and your child is currently at a private nursery that doesn't offer funded places, as it may well be a more flexible and economical option, which will allow you to make the most of your funding.

What about nannies?

Nannies are not Ofsted registered, so you can't use your early learning funding to help you pay for one. They can, however, choose to go on the voluntary part of Ofsted's General Childcare Register and, if they do, you may be able to get financial help in the form of Working Tax Credits or employer-supported childcare vouchers. If your child is looked after by a nanny, she can help you to make the most of your free early learning place by taking and collecting your little one from a nursery for you.

Picking the right provider

Once you've worked out which sort of setting will suit you and your child best, you can find out about the quality of care and learning on offer by checking out the conclusions drawn by Ofsted (or equivalent, if you're in Scotland, Wales, or Northern Ireland). You can ask the provider to see its most recent report, or look on the Ofsted website (see page 196). For a more informal view, ask around and see what other parents think – if you don't actually know anyone with a child there, take a look at, or post on, the local forums at Netmums. And once you've made a choice, make sure you pay a visit to get a feel for the place and the people in charge, and ask lots of questions before signing up. There's a checklist of the sort of things you could ask when you are choosing your childcare in an appendix at the back of the book and there's more information on childcare and pre-school choices on the website of the Daycare Trust (see page 196).

What the netmums say

Pre-school options

I was really happy with the private nursery Natasha was attending for two days a week from the age of eight months, but I wanted to make the most of the free nursery place – especially as one was available at the nursery attached to the primary school we wanted her to go to, and although we were told it wouldn't mean a preferential place at the school, I still felt it might be an advantage. It took quite a bit of reorganising but was quite possible, as I work from home. It was quite a wrench, though, to take her away from friends and carers she'd known practically all her life.

Helen from Harrow, mum to Natasha, five

Both my girls went to the nursery attached to our preferred primary school and it was fab – they got to go to assemblies at the main school, played in the playground, visited classrooms, and so on. In fact, they were used to the general hustle and bustle before they even started school.
Nicola from Edinburgh, mum to Hannah, eight, and Feena, six

Playgroup was a fantastic preparation for school, especially in terms of social development and how to act in a classroom – sitting down, quiet time, free play, eating lunch with friends. They also organised feeder days with the primary school which, although not linked, is in the same catchment area. Having the Reception teachers visiting was a really nice, gentle introduction to school.
Kerry from Cambridge, mum to Theo, five

My son didn't get all his five sessions at our pre-school of choice until the last term, which is an awful waste of what we were entitled to in terms of session funding. As we used a childminder for one day, too, I didn't want to enrol him in another pre-school as it would have been too much – plus I'd taken this approach with his elder brother and I think being part-time at both meant that he didn't settle so well at either. We would have liked to use the full entitlement but we managed and Reuben is a happy lad who has clearly benefited from his time at pre-school. However, I'm disappointed when it's reported that parents choose not to take the full grant. Sometimes the places just aren't there to be used.
Jacqui from Leicester, mum to Zachary, nine, and Reuben, six

I was working part-time (three full days a week) at the time when I could have sent Gemma to pre-school but it just

wasn't practical as the sessions are so short and I had to travel half an hour to work and back. I kept Gemma at a private nursery from one until she started school, although I did receive the funding towards the nursery for the two and a half hour sessions per week, but this didn't go far. She really enjoyed nursery so it wasn't a problem, but looking back it would have been better if the sessions at the local pre-school were longer so I could have sent her there and she could have started to get to know the school environment and meet friends that would go up to school with her. The pre-school is now offering longer days, so we just missed out.
Tanya from St Albans, mum to Gemma, six

I'd heard how important it was to get a nursery place at our preferred primary school, but with my husband and me both working full-time, we didn't know how we'd manage to take it up. Luckily my husband was able to change his hours so that he went into work later after dropping Leila into nursery in the mornings and I negotiated with my boss to let me come in early and work through lunch to leave early. My mum picked Leila up from nursery and kept her until mid-afternoon each day for me. It worked well but I think my mum was glad it was only for a relatively short time, while she was at nursery, as it was a big commitment. When Leila got her school place we were thrilled and we're keeping to the same arrangement with our working hours. I get home in time to collect her from school myself at 3.15pm.
Dolores from Southampton, mum to Leila, five

Is your little one dry?

Some pre-school settings require your child to be out of nappies before starting, while others are more flexible – it's likely to depend on what they've got in the way of staff and facilities. If you need to, check their policy or ask a member of staff.

Don't leave me!

Some children take to a new pre-school setting with no qualms at all, others find settling in a tricky business. You may be upset if your little one cries and clings to you when the time comes to drop her off, but your best bet is to say a firm goodbye and leave. The staff should be well used to dealing with sobbing children, and should be happy to soothe and distract her for you. In most cases, the tears will dry soon after you leave. However, don't be surprised if the fraught goodbyes go on for some weeks or even months. They will almost always settle down eventually.

If your little one has never spent much time apart from you, it's a good idea to ease her in gently. Most nurseries, pre-schools and childminders will suggest at least one short taster session, perhaps inviting you to stick around for a while at first. But even before then, be sure to give your child a chance to spend time without you – if she hasn't already – by leaving her with a good friend or close relative.

Being able to recognise at least a few faces among her fellow attendees should also help with settling, so if she doesn't already have a friend who'll be there at the same time, try to instigate an introduction to one. You may be able to do this through the staff, perhaps by passing on an open invitation to an informal play session or coffee morning. Other mums will be in the same position and will very likely be glad you asked.

There's more on settling issues in Chapter 5.

What the Netmums say

Leaving your little one behind

I was a full-time mum and so pre-school was James' first time away from me, apart from time at his grandparents'. He absolutely loved it from the start and barely stopped to say goodbye. I was the one in tears because he didn't seem to miss me, but I soon got over that and started enjoying the time I had for myself.

Nicola from Walkeringham, mum to James, eleven

Because I am lucky enough to work from home, pre-school was the first experience of childcare outside the home for both of my two. I had two totally different and unexpected experiences! With Thomas I was ready for all the horror stories I had heard about the tears and having to drag them off you... but no, he went in without a backward glance, had a fantastic time from day one, and I have never had a day yet where he hasn't wanted to go to school. Expecting the same with Madeleine, who I thought was a much more confident child, I had continual settling problems all through pre-school. So my advice would be that you really have to wait and see what happens and try and go with the flow, because every child is individual.

Nikki from Carshalton, mum to Thomas, nine, and Madeleine, six

My eldest settled easily at pre-school and loved it from day one. For my youngest child things were completely different. She has always been more cuddly and needed to be close to me. For her, separation was really hard (and for me, too). She didn't have a friend starting with her and found the whole set up of new children and new grown-ups very scary. I would stay with her and encourage her to play but she would always stay right by my side and when I left (ensuring her it was for only half an hour), she would cry and cling and have to be peeled from me. Both of us found this really, really hard and I am sure she knew I was close to tears and anxious, which really didn't help.
Nicola from Edinburgh, mum to Hannah, eight, and Feena, six

It was quite a traumatic experience for both him and me! He was hysterical as I left him and then I had a call when I got home to tell me he had stopped crying and to come and get him after an hour and a half to break him in slowly. After a couple of weeks he started to settle and, in the end, enjoyed going. When it was time for Amy to start she went straight in without a backward glance because she had seen Ben go in and get picked up each day so it was easier for her to settle.
Ali from Burton on Trent, mum to Ben, eight, and Amy, six

If something isn't right . . .

Try not to act rashly if there's something about your child's pre-school care that worries you: perhaps you don't feel the staff are doing their job right, or your little one seems persistently unhappy there for no clear reason. In the first instance, have a polite chat with whoever's in charge: chances are, it's a situation that can be resolved with a little extra communication and, if they're following the requirements of the EYFS, they should be prepared to listen and take action if needed. You can ask about their complaints procedure if you're truly unhappy.

If a problem refuses to go away, or your child really does not seem able to settle, you may simply have to look at trying out a new provider. In this case, you might be able to get your funded place transferred, but this is up to individual local authorities, so you'll have to contact them to ask.

You're a teacher, too

However much of an education your little one's getting outside her home, what she gets inside it matters, too. One very important conclusion of the EPPE Project (see page 2) was that parental attitudes to home learning are *also* a vital factor in development: so doing things like reading with your child, teaching her songs, reciting nursery rhymes and the alphabet, painting and drawing, playing number games, visiting the library, going on interesting outings, and arranging plenty of play dates will all help her to do well in her education a bit later on.

There are lots more good ideas for enjoyable ways to help your child's early learning on the Pre-school Learning Alliance website (see page 195).

What next?

Once your child is happily settled in a pre-school setting, you'll no doubt be turning your thoughts to the next stage. It's certainly a good idea to start thinking about schools once your child is three, if you haven't already. There's all you need to know in the following chapter.

2 Finding the right school

What you need to know

Before you begin the search for a school, you'll no doubt want to know a bit about how the primary education system works generally; what different types of school have to offer and the factors that might influence your choice; and how to go about the application process. It's all outlined below.

How education differs across the UK

Primary education in England is overseen by the Department for Education (formed in May 2010 after the change in government, it replaced the Department for Children, Schools and Families). At a local level the local authorities (LAs) – sometimes more specifically referred to as local education authorities (LEAs) – take responsibility for implementing policy for public education and state schools. LAs vary greatly in size from area to area, with some overseeing as few as 50 schools while others have responsibility for around 500. Full-time education is compulsory for all children aged between five and sixteen.

In Wales, the primary education system operates in a similar way, but the teaching of the Welsh language is compulsory and is used as the primary language for teaching in many schools. The introduction of the Foundation Phase for three- to seven-year-olds is also creating further differences with the system in England.

The system in Northern Ireland is slightly different from elsewhere in the UK, though not as different as it is in Scotland. In Northern Ireland a child's age on 1 July is the key factor in deciding the point of entry into the school system, whereas in England and Wales it is the child's age on 1 September that counts.

In Scotland, the system differs radically from the rest of the UK. They have their own Curriculum for Excellence and children can start at nursery as soon as they reach the age of three, progressing to Primary 1 in the August of the year in which they turn five, although parents of children born between September and February (who are still four years old on the school start date) can elect to keep their child out of school if they do not feel they are ready.

Term dates and holidays

The dates for school terms and holidays are set by a school's LA or, in the case of other types of publicly funded schools, including foundation schools and voluntary-aided schools, by the governing body. In most cases, the school year is divided into three terms, although some LAs have introduced a year with six terms, each of similar length. (This is known as the 'Standard School Year'.)

The National Curriculum

Introduced in 1988 to ensure that all state schools were consistent in what they taught, the National Curriculum is a statutory framework that lays out all the requirements of your child's education. It's made up of blocks of years known as Key Stages: Key Stage 1 covers school Years 1 and 2 (in other words, your child's education from age five to seven); while Key Stage 2 covers school Years 3 to 6 (in other words, your child's education from age seven to eleven). So together Key Stages 1 and 2 make up the primary curriculum. The Early Years Foundation Stage (see page 4) is also part of the National Curriculum – it covers care and education from birth to five, and includes your child's pre-schooling and her first year at school, which is known as Reception. And later, beyond primary school, your child will move through Key Stage 3 (Years 7 to 9) and Key Stage 4 (Years 10 and 11, which takes them up to the age of sixteen).

The National Curriculum includes a number of compulsory subjects. During Key Stages 1 and 2, these are English; maths; science; design and technology; information and communication technology (ICT); history; geography; art and design; music; and physical education. Schools also have to teach religious education (RE) – although you have the right to withdraw your child from these lessons – and are advised to teach Personal, Social, Health and Economic (PSHE) education and citizenship, together with at least one modern foreign language.

National Curriculum Assessments take place at several points while your child is at school. Often known as Standard Assessment Testing, or SATS, these assessments have proved controversial since being introduced, with many teachers claiming that they put children under unnecessary stress and lead to a league-table-obsessed culture in schools. In fact, they have already been scrapped at the end of Key Stage 3 (Year 9) and – at the time of writing – many teachers are still threatening to boycott those at the end of Key Stage 2 (Year 6). The tests your little one will sit at the end of Key Stage 1 (in other words, at the end of Year 2, when he is aged seven, or very soon to be) are based on teacher assessment and include writing, speaking, listening, maths and science.

There's a bit more about the National Curriculum on page 18, and more about what it will mean for your child in his first year at school on page 134. There's also lots of further information about it on the website of the Qualifications and Curriculum Development Agency (see page 197).

About Ofsted

Ofsted (Office for Standards in Education, Children's Services and Skills) is a government department which was set up in 1992 to inspect and regulate institutions in England which provide education to learners of all ages, as well as providers of care for children and young people, and to effect improvements within these sectors.

All state schools must undergo inspection by Ofsted at least every three years, after which it publishes a report which is available to the public. There's more about Ofsted reports on page 41.

Inspection and regulation elsewhere in the UK

Wales, Scotland and Northern Ireland all have their own equivalents to Ofsted: in Wales it is Estyn (with a separate body, the Care and Social Services Inspectorate for Wales, responsible for early years care); in Scotland it is Her Majesty's Inspectorate for Education (with responsibility for early years care coming under the Care Commission); and in Northern Ireland it is the Department of Education Northern Ireland. Details for all of these are at the back of the book.

School-starting age

Although the law states that children must be in full-time education from the term following their fifth birthday (known as statutory school age), most schools now have a Reception class, which takes children from the term after their fourth birthday. Many Reception classes have a single intake, with all children beginning in September. However, to allow for the fact that some four-year-olds with a birthday late in the academic year might not be ready to start school, some offer two separate starts – one at the beginning of the autumn term, in September, and one at the start of the spring term, in January. A few schools even have a third intake, at the start of the summer term, in April. Some get around the age gap discrepancy by starting off the younger ones on a part-time basis, perhaps for as much as a term or more.

Ready to start school at four?

If your four-year-old isn't due to turn five until comparatively late in the school year and he's joining a single intake in September, you may feel that's he's too young and will be disadvantaged against his older peers. After all, at that age, when development is still rapidly taking place, it's a gap that can make quite a difference. It may be that he's bright enough to cope with things academically but is emotionally young; or he may be emotionally mature yet find it hard to grasp certain elements of his learning. You might simply be worried that he'll be too tired to make it through a long school day.

Technically you have the right to defer his entry to a spring or summer start. (You may even think he's too young to start that year at all and would prefer that he misses out Reception altogether and begins his formal schooling in Year 1: you're also within your rights to take this option, since a child does not have to begin until the term *after* his fifth birthday.)

If you're considering deferment as a possibility, bear in mind that you will still need to apply at the expected time (for more on the application process see page 55). And be sure to discuss it with the school or admissions authority – some parents report being told they risk losing a place altogether after making such a request. And do weigh up the potential disadvantages of deferment as well as any benefits. The argument against it is that your child could miss out on opportunities to form friendships, or the chance for a nice, long, gentle transition period to the more formal education of Year 1. And, of course, it means delaying your own release from the demands of caring for – or finding childcare for – an active pre-schooler.

Another option is to request part-time hours, if this isn't something the school already offers (and many do). If it's a compromise you feel could work well, then it's worth suggesting it to the head, or Reception teacher.

Meanwhile, you might want to be on hand with some extra support if your child is among the younger half of his class. Firstly, be sure to have a chat about it with his teacher – they should be able to give you reassurance that they'll be making allowances for his young age. At home, you can help him practise the skills he's learning at school through play: with word games, for instance, or letting him help count pieces of fruit into a bag at the shops, socks in and out of the washing machine, or coins in a pile of loose change (although this goes for helping children of any age – there are more ideas on making learning fun and offering support from home in Chapter 6). Keep your own expectations in check – don't be tempted to compare his achievements to his peers or his siblings at the same stage of their school career. And most of all, give him loads of praise and reassurance – although, that's also good advice, whatever the age of your child.

> ***Emma says:*** Summer-born children can find starting school a little more challenging than their older peers – it needs to be remembered that some may only have made it into that academic year by a matter of days or hours. It can be harder socially and academically, or it might be that they're simply

too tired to manage full-time schooling. The Early Years Foundation Stage means that each child should be receiving the support and learning experiences they need to make progress, so any good Reception teacher will be very aware of these hurdles and put strategies in place to help – adapting their teaching and activities to suit the individual child. They also need to monitor self-esteem in the child, who may notice that they're not progressing with their learning as quickly as their older classmates. Parents need to be aware of the potential differences as they may worry that their child seems to be behind, or is struggling in some way.

What the Netmums say

Ready to start school?

Our first son, Lewis, was born in February, so we were very happy for him to start school in the January just before he was five. He was more than ready and getting a bit bored with all the mum-and-toddler groups we'd been going to. Our second boy, Callum, was born in August, so he will be able to start school a month after he turns four, but we've decided to wait until the following year. He's not as easily bored as Lewis was and seems less mature than his brother was at the same stage. Also, because I now know how things are taught in school I can give him a head start if he seems ready earlier.
Lena from Norwich, mum to Lewis, six, and Callum, three

My twins were born in June. Janesh thrived when he started school in September at just four and a quarter, but Ranjiv was

far less happy and took the whole of the first term to settle in. It's tricky when you have two children the same age but at different stages. We felt we didn't have much choice than to send them both together as they are pretty inseparable.
Ayesha from London, mum to Janesh and Ranjiv, four

Nina's the eldest in her class – she was virtually five when she started school – and she's bright, too, so she was more than ready for it. She absolutely thrived from the minute she walked through the door.
Julia from Milton Keynes, mum to Nina, seven, and Ellie, four

My daughter is a summer child so started in January. It was quite hard at first as the new kids were given very little time to settle and she had to catch up quickly, with a new book to read every day for the first two months. Also making friends was harder, as all the September starters had already paired up. She's the youngest in the class with many of her classmates almost a year older. But she seems happy enough now.
Sharon from Preston, mum to Anne-Marie, five

Beginning your search

For some parents, it's never too soon to look at the possible options for a first school – in fact, in these competitive times, couples have been known to relocate even before their child is born to ensure they're in the 'right' catchment area! But even if the issue doesn't crop up quite as soon as that, it's not too early to start thinking about schools once your child is three, since it's usual now for children to begin school within the year after turning four. Bear in mind, too, that local authorities set early deadlines for applications, with some as much as a whole year ahead of when your child is due to start.

One word of warning if you *are* thinking well ahead: do be wary of moving house purely because it will put you near a favoured school. For one thing, standards in schools can very easily change – either way – over a few short years. And, for another, it's a good idea to be realistic: after all, no child is *guaranteed* a place at the school of their parents' choosing. So moving house to be near a 'good' school won't *definitely* get you in.

Getting your child's 'name down' on a list (at this stage) won't stand you in good stead, either: all you can do in advance of admission age is to register your interest with a school, and all that will ensure is that you'll get an information and/or application pack when the time comes.

Dr Bob says: Making the decision to move house in order to get your child into the 'right' school is a huge step and not one to be taken lightly. A family should always give the most careful consideration to all possible outcomes, including knock-on effects such as travel to work and possible unrealistic expectations. Schools do not stand still: the hope is that they will continue not only to live up to a good reputation but to improve. Unfortunately, though, this isn't always the case.

What the netmums say

Planning ahead when picking a school

I went to the local village primary myself and, although I moved away to a big city for my twenties, I decided to move

back when I found I was pregnant with Thomas. The school has kept its good reputation and there are so few of us in the village and surrounding areas that there's never a problem getting a child in. It reassures me a great deal that Thomas is enjoying the school, too – and knowing I went there before means it already feels familiar to him.
Alice from Cheltenham, mum to Thomas, four

We moved house when our son was two years old in order to get into the catchment area for the school of our choice. To a degree, we were affected by the bigger picture of high-school applications, as the primary school we chose is a feeder school for the local grammar school.
Ruth from Lancaster, mum to Jamie, four

We moved towns purely so my children could go to better schools. I had been living in what was classed as a deprived area for many years and, before the children came along, it didn't particularly bother us. We moved back to my home town when Lucy was a newborn so she and her sister could go to the primary and secondary schools that I went to: I knew they still had good reputations as my nephews attended them. My poor husband has to travel 40 miles a day to work as a result, but I'm glad we moved.
Jo from Leicester, mum to Faye, four, and Lucy, two

We didn't give a second thought to local schools when we moved house – even though I was pregnant at the time! I suppose I was terribly naïve, but the whole borough is renowned for its schools so it just didn't cross my mind. I knew we had a good chance of getting Nicola into the local Catholic primary, as I am a practising Catholic, but I hadn't

> even considered over-subscription being a problem. One of the criteria is how far you live from the school, so it was a big relief to find that it is only seven minutes' walk away, and so we scored the necessary points for that. More by luck than judgement, I have to say.
> *Judith from Bristol, mum to Nicola, five*

Looking into your options

If you've lived in your area a while, chances are you already know where the local primary schools are. But if you're not sure where to find them, a good place to start is the Direct Gov website's school finder (there's a link to this page listed in the back of the book). It allows you to search online by typing in your postcode and provides a profile of all state schools in your area. You can also ask your local authority for a free publication outlining details of the schools (the schools themselves will usually have a copy available, too).

If you find the thought of the whole process a bit bewildering, find out from your local authority if there's a Choice Advice Service in your area, offering impartial guidance and help in understanding the system, either over the phone or face-to-face. There's also lots of good stuff on the Advisory Centre for Education's website (see page 196).

Once you know what your options are, make sure you get hold of a prospectus for any school you're interested in. These are likely to provide a valuable mine of information: typically they'll tell you about admission policies, ethos, how the curriculum is covered, policies on special needs and pastoral care, uniform requirements, school hours and a summary of what Ofsted says about the school in question. With most schools boasting a website these days, you may also find what you need on the internet.

Don't assume you only need to look at one school because it's the one you want. Look at as many as you practically can, then list them in order of preference so you're ready to complete the application form when the time comes.

Schools explained

If you're confused about the many different types of schools that are around, you're not alone. Here's a bit more information to help you make sense of it all.

State schools

It's more than likely that your child will be attending a state school. Every child has the right to a free place at one of these between the ages of five and sixteen. These are also known sometimes as maintained schools since they are financed, or maintained, by local authorities.

Generally speaking the state school system has two tiers: primary and secondary. At primary level, schools may cater just for infants (aged four to seven) or juniors (aged seven to eleven), or they may have all these age groups in one school. Where they are split into two, it will mean making two separate applications, even if the junior school feeds from the infant school.

However, in a few areas of the country a three-tier system operates and usually this comprises a first, or lower, school that covers Reception to Year 4 (ages four to nine); a middle school covering Years 5 to 7 (ages nine to twelve); and an upper or high school covering Years 8 to 11 (ages twelve to sixteen). This system has both fans and critics. Those in favour of it say that having three phases means there isn't a huge leap between primary school and secondary school for children to contend with; the opposing argument is that children are too young to enter the relatively mature environment of middle school at the start of Year 5.

Community schools

Community schools are a kind of state school and are run by the local authority, who employs all staff, owns the land and buildings, and lays down the admissions criteria (special conditions used to allocate places in the event of over-subscription). Some community schools forge strong links with the local community by offering childcare services and, in some cases, adult learning classes. They may also make their facilities available to the wider community.

Foundation schools

Foundation schools are run by their own governing body, which is responsible for employing staff and laying down the admissions criteria. The land and school buildings may either be owned by the governing body or by a charitable foundation.

Trust schools

A type of foundation school, trust schools form a charitable trust with an external partner, such as an educational charity or a business, with a view to raising standards or finding new ways of working.

Voluntary-aided schools

Usually religious (or 'faith') schools, although non-faith schools can also apply to become voluntary aided, this type of school operates in a similar way to foundation schools, with staff employed by the governing body, which also lays down the admissions criteria. The land and buildings are normally owned by a charitable foundation, often a religious organisation, and the governing body contributes to the maintenance of the school.

Voluntary-controlled schools

Voluntary-controlled schools operate in a similar way to voluntary-aided schools, in that the buildings and land are usually owned by a charitable body, often a religious organisation. This body also appoints some of the school governors. Where they differ is that voluntary-controlled schools are run by the local authority, which employs staff and lays down admissions criteria.

Specialist schools

You may have heard of high schools gaining 'specialist' status in certain learning areas and currently the scheme is being trialled in some primary schools, so it's worth asking if your shortlisted schools are either part of the scheme or planning to work towards specialist status if the pilot scheme gets rolled out across all primaries. Specialist schools follow the National Curriculum but get extra funding to spend on staff, training and equipment in their specialist area and must develop a strategy for raising standards in that particular field. Specialist areas include music, modern languages, art, science and sports.

Community and foundation special schools

These cater for children with specific special educational needs, including physical disabilities or learning difficulties.

Faith schools

Faith schools are mostly run in the same way as other state schools, following the National Curriculum. The faith status, however, means that priority is usually given to those children whose families can produce evidence of their adherence to the faith, and many faith schools are over-subscribed. Because of over-subscription, faith schools usually dictate their own admissions criteria. The curriculum and staffing policies may also reflect their faith status. Faith schools can be Roman Catholic, Anglican, Jewish, Church of England, Muslim and, less prevalently, Sikh, Greek Orthodox and Seventh Day Adventist (of which there is currently only one in the UK).

When applying to a faith school, you may need a reference from a priest, minister, rabbi or other cleric, and/or a baptismal certificate as proof of commitment to the faith. However, some faith schools also admit a percentage of non-religious pupils – if you don't worship but you'd like to consider a local faith school as an option, it's worth checking its policy before ruling it out.

Academies

Academies are state-funded schools that operate outside of local authority control and have more freedom in how they're governed, how much the teachers are paid and what is taught. Currently, only secondary schools can be academies but plans for new legislation means that primaries will be invited to apply for academy status, too.

Free schools

Similar to academies, free schools are run independently but with state funding. They offer charities, trusts, voluntary groups and even parents, the chance to set up and run their own schools.

Independent or private schools

Independent or private schools receive no grants from public funds and are owned and managed under special trusts. They are either pre-preparatory, for ages two to seven, or junior or preparatory ('prep') schools, for ages seven to eleven or thirteen. (Prep schools use the last two years in the school to prepare pupils for the Common Entrance exam, which they must pass in order to gain entry to an independent secondary school.) Some fee-charging schools are privately owned and run for profit; others are charitable foundations. Some offer boarding; others are day schools. The Independent Schools Information Service (ISIS) offers a guide giving the names and addresses of schools, along with their entry requirements. Independent schools are either Ofsted-inspected or monitored by an inspectorate approved by the Secretary of State.

There are pros and cons to private schools. Class sizes tend to be smaller so that there is greater focus on each individual child; they tend to follow a broader curriculum and demonstrate very good results – typically around 20% higher at the end of Key Stage 2 than their state counterparts – but the costs may be prohibitive. Children in private schools are likely to be rubbing shoulders with only other privileged individuals, too, and this is something to consider if you would prefer your child to meet and mingle with all social groups. Because parents are paying for their children's education, the emphasis is usually on high achievement, with the atmosphere often more studious and disciplined than state schools – not a bad thing, you may argue, but not necessarily the best environment for every child.

The Independent Schools Council gives the average cost per term of an independent primary day school (from age three to eleven) as £3,180 and, at three terms a year, that comes to £9,540. School trips and extra-curricular activities can push the cost up by as much as an extra 10% and the cost of uniform is very likely to be steep. Some schools offer bursaries (help with fees) and these are awarded subject to means testing.

Alternative independent primary schools

There are 31 Steiner-Waldorf schools and 56 early years settings in the UK and Ireland, all of which are fee-paying. Children enter kindergarten at age three and the philosophy is that they don't start formal school or have formal lessons in numeracy and literacy until age seven. The emphasis is on the development of the whole child, with particular stress given to creative, social and spiritual values. Currently there are issues with this philosophy, as all providers of early years education are obliged to offer the Early Years Foundation Stage (EYFS). Almost all the schools are applying for exemption, but the process is lengthy and somewhat complicated.

There are 631 registered Montessori nursery and primary schools in the UK, all of which are fee-paying. (The Montessori Association is planning to launch the first-ever state Montessori school, using its own finances for setting up, plus extra funding either from a local authority or private sponsor.) The Montessori philosophy is based on the belief that children go through various sensitive stages in which they are very receptive to learning specific skills. Montessori students are allowed to learn at their own pace, with little whole-class teaching offered. They can spend as much or as little time on a topic as they want, the idea being that they will intuitively direct their own development.

There are also some one-off schools up and down the UK offering a more holistic approach to learning. You'll find them online when you search for 'alternative primary education'.

Home education

You are obliged by law to make sure your child is educated but there is an alternative to sending them to school and that's teaching them at home. It's something a small number of parents choose to do, perhaps because they feel they're best able to identify their own child's needs and learning preferences, or they prefer the flexibility that home schooling offers. Some may consider it as their only option if they've been unable to secure a place at a school they're happy with.

Parents don't have to be qualified teachers to home school their child and you don't have to get special permission from your local authority or even inform them of your intention – although it is wise to do so. However, the law requires you to ensure your child receives the equivalent of a full-time education suitable to their age, ability and aptitude, and to recognise and respond to any special educational needs your child may have. Other than that, the arrangement is pretty flexible. You don't have to stick to school hours, days or terms, or to follow the National Curriculum or put your child through national tests. It's worth bearing in mind that there are no funds directly available from central government for home schooling, so you need to be sure you can afford to pursue this option.

Special needs

If your child has a disability or a statement of special educational needs (SEN), then you have a right to opt for either a mainstream or special school. Your local authority must comply, as long as the school you choose is suitable for your child's age, ability, skills and SEN; your child meets any required academic selection criteria (usually not applicable for state schools); your child's presence will not have a negative impact on the education of other children already at the school; or placing your child in the school will be an efficient use of the local authority's resources.

Some schools cater for certain needs but not others, so you must be clear about what your child's requirements actually are. For example, your chosen school may have good access for physically disabled pupils or cater well for children with dyslexia, but not be equipped for partially sighted or deaf pupils. If in doubt, ask to see the school's policy on disability and SEN to make sure they can offer what your child needs. You should make a school visit to any shortlisted special school just as you would to a mainstream school.

You also have the choice of selecting a school that is not run by your local authority; for example, a non-maintained special school (usually run by charities), an independent school that can meet your child's needs, or a school maintained by another local authority. However, the local authority has no legal duty to send your child to a non-maintained or independent school if there's a suitable state school with a place available.

Dr Bob says: The current thinking among educational theorists is that children with special or 'additional' needs will benefit most from inclusion with children not manifesting these needs. There's a strong philosophical case for this thinking, but in practice there can be a lack of the resources necessary to make it work. Do check that the positive message of inclusion can be matched by the quality of supportive provision on offer.

Assessing schools . . . and drawing up your shortlist

You're very likely to be looking at more than one possibility when it comes to picking a primary school and, when it comes to drawing up a shortlist of preferences, there's a whole load of potential considerations to make. The main ones are outlined on the next page – some may represent vital criteria for you, others may be less important or not important at all, at least at this early stage (although you may want to know a bit more about them, for your own information, once your application has been successful).

Remember, it is sensible not to get your heart pinned on a specific school, if you can help it. Have at least one other on your shortlist that you would be happy with.

Will we get in?

Of course, it has to be said that lots of parents *do* set their hearts on one particular school. But, before you do – especially if it's a popular one – you should consider the possibility that you won't *definitely* get a place there, however much you want one. Demand for schools can vary a lot from area to area and some schools become oversubscribed – in other words, they have more children who apply than there are places for.

When this happens, oversubscription criteria will be used as a basis to allocate places. These criteria are set by the admission authority who – depending on the type of school – can be either the local authority or the governing body and who must comply with a set of rules known as the Schools Admissions Code. They vary, so you'll need to find out from schools themselves, or from the local authority, what they are and whether you can fulfil them. But typically, they could include whether your child has a sibling already attending the school; catchment area, or your proximity to the school; whether your child has special needs; and, in the case of faith schools, evidence of commitment to the faith served by the school. In most schools it's normal for priority to be given to looked-after children – in other words those living with a foster carer or in a children's home.

The right school? Issues you may want to consider when choosing

Its location

In an ideal world, you'll live nice and close to the primary school your child attends. For one thing, proximity to your home or being in the catchment area is very often among admission criteria. But not only that, being able to walk to school is a massive bonus because you'll save on petrol and keep your carbon footprint low. You won't have to waste precious time sitting in traffic, getting in and out of the car (especially tedious if you've got younger ones and you need to lug car seats or pushchairs around), or finding a parking space. And, of course, it's much healthier for you and your child. Another benefit is that you're likely to be living near other children who attend, which will make socialising out of school that much easier.

If you work and your job is more than a walk away and you need to get there straight after the school run, how you're going to manage that in the time you've got is likely to be a consideration. You might even choose a school that's near, or on the way to, your job to help you with this. Or it may be that you need to look at schools which are close to your child's care provider, if they will be the person who takes and/or collects them from school. (There's more about that in Chapter 4.)

You aren't restricted to applying to schools within your borough or county: in theory, you can send your child to school anywhere.

Its ethos

High up on your list of features in a school, no doubt, will be its ethos. It's hard to define what a school's ethos is but a whole load of important aspects will be encompassed in it: its values, climate and outlook; attitudes of and relationships between staff and pupils; and methods of dealing with matters such as behaviour management, accidents and bullying.

Many schools publish what's known as an ethos statement in their prospectus which outlines its outlook, but as these are just words, you can only get a really good idea about a school's ethos by gauging opinions from other parents, asking staff the right questions, and spending at least some time there for yourself and soaking up the atmosphere.

You might like to look, for instance, at its approach to discipline – some schools operate a 'whole school' approach, where all the staff follow the same line and the children are in no doubt as to the consequences of bad behaviour. Others allow for different teachers to use their own approach, which often means that the children respond better to some teachers and support staff than to others. Look for examples of 'positive discipline' when you visit the school. (Teachers who use positive discipline will say: 'Half the class is sitting with arms folded: thank you, well done'; rather than, 'Why are half of you still not sitting with arms folded?')

Another element of a school's ethos you might want to investigate is how they'll comfort your child if he becomes upset or ill while at school – you may find that staff abide by advice from the teaching unions to avoid physical contact wherever possible, which could mean he won't get a cuddle or any other sort of physical comfort if he needs it. (Some schools and individual teachers – particularly those in charge of Reception – remain relaxed about this guideline, though, and are happy to dish out a hug if required).

You might also find out how the school encourages children who find it hard to make friends (with a 'buddy' system, for example); how staff will address any concerns you may have and what its anti-bullying policy involves (it is compulsory by law to have measures in place that prevent and tackle bullying if it arises). There's more on these subjects in Chapter 5.

Emma says: The ethos in a school is its passion, its spirit, its attitude and its focus. It is the heartbeat that runs through it and should be strong, focused and ambitious. Any school can write about their ethos, but in a good school they will live and breathe it in all they do. It is not a statement, it's an action. The ethos of the school should be all around you when you visit. You should be able to get a true sense of the school from displays, listening to staff, meeting pupils and chatting to other parents. Meeting the head is a really good way of judging how true the school's ethos claims are. A head should always be leading by example.

What other parents say

Positive feedback from other parents is always worth having. If you don't already have some parents in your social circle who you can tap for opinions, you could go to the local discussion boards on Netmums and post your questions there. Ask about the pros and cons as they see them, but remember that other people's feelings will always be subjective. Don't be swayed either way simply because of something someone's told you: find out for yourself.

You'll probably want to compare notes with parents among your child's peer group, too, to find out where their children are going. Having at least one friend that he knows and gets on with – and preferably several – will be a real bonus for your little one when he starts school, so it makes sense to factor this in. And having some familiar faces among the parents at the gates, and some friends to swap notes with, will be reassuring for you, too.

Emma says: You may find it useful to speak to other parents who have children at your local schools. They will often give you a very honest account of their experiences; the way that the school communicates with parents, teaching styles and whether or not their children have been happy there. Do remember, though, that all children are different, so what suits their children may not necessarily suit yours.

What Ofsted says

You'll get a good overview of a school by looking at the outcome of its most recent Ofsted reports. You can get a copy from the school, or read it on its website; or you can go direct to the Ofsted website. (If you live in Wales, Scotland or Northern Ireland, you will need to go to the site of the equivalent body – see page 20.) Bear in mind that inspections take place every three years, so don't let a less-than-glowing report from a couple of years back put you off visiting the school, or assume that a fantastic report means standards are being maintained: a lot can happen in the years between inspections – that's the point of them.

Typically, inspectors give only two days' notice before visiting a school, then spend two days analysing its performance. The exam results will have been noted prior to the inspection. During the visit, the inspector will talk to staff and pupils to gain insights into the school's ethos, curriculum, effectiveness and education standards. In some cases, parents' comments will have been collated, too. Ofsted inspectors aren't just looking for academic excellence, though: they're also very keen to gauge how well schools are doing in terms of encouraging personal development; monitoring individuals' progress; building confidence; pastoral care;

standards of behaviour; happiness of the children; incidence of bullying and truanting; and provision of quality equipment.

Ploughing through one or more Ofsted reports can seem like a laborious task, but you can save time by focusing on the important bits. A good place to start is with the overall score of the school: 1 = Outstanding; 2 = Good; 3 = Satisfactory; and 4 = Inadequate. Then you can read the summary of the analysis, looking for terms like 'rapidly improving' if the school doesn't seem to be performing well overall.

If a school has been placed in 'special measures' it means that it's failing to meet government requirements for education and is severely under-performing.

Achievement and attainment tables

You can also get an idea of a primary school's academic attainment levels by looking at Key Stage 2 achievement and attainment tables (also known as performance tables and often just as league tables), where applicable, which show how well pupils have done in their National Curriculum assessments and which rank schools according to outcome. You can access these via the Department of Education website, but they are also published in national newspapers.

Don't for a moment consider league tables the be-all and end-all, though. They only reflect academic results and may be influenced by the overall ability of the children in each school's intake, or bolstered by parents who are prepared to pay for out-of-school tuition. They don't necessarily reflect the standard of teaching and they certainly won't inform you how happy your child is likely to be at a school, or how well they will fare individually. However, if a school has a consistently low achievement record, with little or no movement in results from year to year, you may want to find out why.

Its size . . . and the size of its classes

There are pros and cons to weigh up when it comes to looking at the size of a school. A smaller school, if one's available in your area, may suit your child better if he's quite shy or reticent, or if he is easily fazed by crowds. A larger school, on the other hand, might suit a gregarious child as there will be more opportunities to mix with different children and perhaps more choice of after-school activities. It will also be less of a contrast when the time eventually comes for the transition to middle or secondary.

A surge in birth rate and a shortage of school places generally has meant that class sizes have grown over the years – the average infant class size in England was 26.2 in January 2009, compared with 25.7 children in 2008. By law, classes in the first three years of primary education cannot have more than 30 children in them, but many teachers feel even that is too many. It's generally felt that the smaller the class size, the more individual attention each child will get, the more likely they are to be able to participate, and the greater the scope for helping those who need most support. However, there's no actual evidence that big classes mean lower standards.

If you are concerned about large classes, you could find out what the teacher has in the way of help, whether from a full- or part-time paid classroom assistant, or regular volunteers. There's more about teaching assistants and their role on page 133.

Starting arrangements

It may be a good idea to find out early on how the schools you're interested in tackle starting arrangements for 'newbies', as policies on this vary a great deal. Most schools offer some sort of staggered start in order to help ease Reception children into school life, which could mean days, weeks, or even a term or more of part-time hours or half days.

Parents' feelings about staggered starts vary. While most would accept it's important for a little one to be gently introduced to full-time schooling, for others it's an inconvenience they could do without. If you work, you'll more than likely need to make special arrangements during this period so you've got all the childcare you need covered. There's a bit more on staggered starts in Chapter 5.

How the staff seem

You'll be putting the care and education of your child largely in the hands of one person – their teacher – so you'll no doubt want to meet that person and satisfy yourself that they seem enthusiastic about their job and that they enjoy working with children. And as a good school will have a good head teacher, you'll probably want to know something about who's in charge overall. The Ofsted report will tell you more about the quality of the leadership and may also comment specifically on who's running the Reception class. Generally speaking, though, meeting and chatting to staff will be the best way to get an idea of what they're like.

Emma says: I would always go on instinct. A good head teacher should be interested in your child. Try to watch them with the other children – does he or she know their names? How do pupils respond to them? You can find out a certain amount from Ofsted reports and, of course, you can also speak to other parents – but if you do that, remember that personality clashes can sometimes cloud judgement.

What they teach there . . . and how

Although schools are bound by the basic framework of the National Curriculum, they may choose to cover these subjects very differently. If you want to, you should be able to find out more about the specifics of how a school interprets the curriculum by checking the prospectus or looking at its website – or simply by chatting to staff. In particular, you may be interested to know about how they cover subjects such as religion and Personal, Social, Health and Economic (PSHE) education.

The emphasis a school puts on academic achievement in the early years may or may not be important to you: some schools are hot on this – for instance, they may have a policy of streaming or setting (streaming is where children are put into different groups according to their general ability, setting is where they are grouped according to ability in different subjects), while others are more laid-back. You might also want to find out about homework and how much your child is likely to be set – government guidelines recommend that schools issue homework, even at primary level, and schools are entitled to decide how much or little they set – you may have a view on this either way! (There's more about homework on page 170.)

If you have a child who has a special educational need – or even if you feel he may need a little extra help – take a close look at the school's educational special needs policy and find out what's on offer in terms of extra support for those who need it. (There's more on special educational needs on page 35.)

You might also want to find out if your chosen schools have a special interest – for instance, some put a strong focus on music, sports, art or drama. What's on offer in terms of extra-curricular activities could also be of significance: subsidised tuition in musical instruments, for example; French classes at lunchtime; or any number of other after-school clubs.

Emma says: If you have a child with diagnosed special needs it's likely that you have been thinking about suitable schools for some time before having to apply. You may need to speak to the professionals involved in your child's care to find out which schools have the facilities and expertise to support your child, and this in turn may further restrict your choice of school.

It's important to visit all your school options and chat to the Special Educational Needs Co-ordinator (SENCO) about how they feel they would be able to support your child. A good school will have systems firmly in place to support children with special educational needs (SEN) and will ensure that you're kept fully informed of your child's progress. It's also a good idea to speak to other parents who have children with SEN to gather their views on how the system at the school works.

If your child is likely to need a Statement of Special Educational Needs [see page 35] then the process for starting school and getting support in place will need to begin about ten months before they start school. You (or your child's pre-school) will need to write to the local authority to ask for a Statutory Assessment. If a Statement is agreed then it becomes a legally binding document which sets out the level of support your child will need.

Environment and facilities

A school that appears to be well equipped, furnished and cared for is very likely to appeal, it's true. By all means check these things out – but bear in mind they are only surface details and won't reflect the standard of teaching, or other highly important factors, such as ethos. A lack of them shouldn't necessarily put you off.

What it offers in the way of extended hours

More and more primary schools are offering 'wrap-around care' now, with breakfast and after-school clubs commonplace, either run by the school itself or an independent provider. For working parents, they can be a real boon as they're usually affordable. It can also offer a good sense of continuity and comfort for a child to be cared for either side of school hours in the same, familiar place. So whether or not extended hours are available – and the quality of care on offer – could certainly be a factor that swings a school in your favour. There's more on this issue on page 105.

The quality of the school that comes next

Some primary schools are what is known as 'feeders' for certain secondary schools (or middle schools, in the case of a three-tier system). This means they'll have close links to the secondary in question, which is likely to give priority to 'fed' children when it comes to allocating places. If you've got designs on a school which you think you'll favour later in their academic career and it's got a feeder, it would make sense to apply to it. (Bearing in mind that it won't necessarily guarantee you a place when the time comes!)

Dr Bob says: When considering issues like the high schools into which primaries feed, it will be as well to remember that these can change quite radically over the six years that your child is attending primary. Try to get a longer-term perspective on whether the high schools' reputations have changed over time, possibly in line with the appointment of a new principal.

Do they mix or shuffle classes?

Some schools operate a policy of mixed-age classes, where, for example, Year 1 and Year 2 are divided up and groups from each put together. An increasing number of schools are adopting the strategy and there are pros and cons. On the plus side, some studies have shown that children thrive better in a learning environment that's similar to a family set-up, with older and younger children in the mix. (The theory is that younger children look up to their older classmates, while older children enjoy the feeling of nurturing the younger ones.) Educationalists have discovered that mixing the ages within a classroom encourages problem-solving skills, empathy, thinking strategies, vocabulary and social interaction; and that older children who are below the expected ability levels for their age may feel less exposed (since mixed-age classes are inevitably made up of mixed ability, too), while the more able younger ones may benefit from being mixed with older peers. Arguments against the mixed-age system include the concern that younger children who aren't reaching expected levels for their age may find the gap between their abilities and those of the oldest children demoralizing; that lesson planning is more complex, with teachers needing to organise small groups of same-ability children for core subjects such as maths and English; and that there can be more problems with discipline in classes where children have differing levels of maturity.

If you're keen on a particular school but unsure about its policy of mixed-age teaching, find out more by arranging to chat with the head teacher, who should be able to explain in depth why the strategy was chosen and how it works for the school.

Class shuffling is another policy favoured in a few schools and one you may have a view on. This is where – in a school with more than one form per year – pupils within the same year group are mixed at certain points, perhaps in between Reception and Year 1, or during the transition from infant to junior. Again, there are pros and cons. On the plus side, children have an opportunity to get to know the whole year group well and have more chances to make new friends or pursue friendships previously enjoyed only at break times; teachers get to know the whole year group; and, if there are any disruptive children, they are shared between the two classes and may respond differently to different teachers. Drawbacks may include your child becoming separated from his best mate or even his whole group of friends and he may find it difficult to make new ones (although, hopefully, the staff will have strategies for rectifying this). Again, this is a policy which you might like to talk to the head about.

What the Netmums say

Where did you look . . . and what were you looking for?

The main consideration for us was proximity. I want my children to live close to the school, to be able to walk there and also to be able to walk to friends' houses. The school we've chosen has a strong sense of community, which I also feel is important for integrating my daughter into the social world.

Anne from Gloucester, mum to Rachael, four

For us, it was a simple choice of two schools, both of which are within a ten-minute walk and boast good reports from Ofsted. We visited each and one just seemed that much nicer, with a head teacher who was vibrant and friendly when we met him. We also had friends with children there, and they thought it was a great school, so that swung it and we put it down as our first choice. Interestingly, it is a Church of England school but it's not a criteria that you worship to go there, which is fortunate, as we're not religious.

Julia from Milton Keynes, mum to Nina, seven, and Ellie, four

The main priorities for us were the facilities (it's a new school), seeing some familiar faces and the fact that we knew people with children there who raved about it.
Katy from Huddersfield, mum to Grace, five, and Oscar, one

We looked at our three nearest schools and, during the process, I made up my mind that the most important aspect of school life for this age group was the relationship between the children and the staff. None of our local schools offered quite the warmth and interaction we were looking for and we ended up sending the boys a bit further afield. It's not too much of a bind because I work from home so I can drop them off and pick them up OK. I'm hoping that some of our local high schools will suit them, though, as I think proximity to home is a major advantage at that point.
Heather from Aylesbury, mum to Luke and Alex, five

I visited three schools when we were looking for Matthew and they were all very different. The one closest to our home had an outstanding Ofsted and people moved house to try and get into the catchment area. The second was on a large estate and had over 25 per cent of children with English as their second language and a turnover of about 30 per cent each term. It had a very good Ofsted. The third was too far to walk, had an average Ofsted, but had by far the most welcoming set up. In the end I chose this one for its friendly, open approach and its mission statement, which is: 'We want every child to enjoy coming to school.' We were offered a place at the first and they got quite shirty when I turned it down. I must be one of the few people not to take up a place there but I have absolutely

no regrets. You need to trust your instincts and go with what is right for your child – not what everyone expects you to want!
Carol from Biggin Hill, mum to Matthew, six

I ended up having to fork out for private education as the state schools in my area were so disappointing, and I really believe the primary education experience sets the scene for a child's later learning. I did consider home schooling, but as a single parent running my own business I needed to continue working full-time and earning. The fees are pretty crippling for me to manage on my own, and it means we don't get to go on holidays abroad, but I think UK camping trips are educational in themselves! I think Emily feels the difference, though, as most of her school friends' families are fairly wealthy, and they come back after the holidays with stories of all these fantastic locations they've visited. Happily, the high schools near us are actually pretty good, so private education is a relatively short-term commitment financially. I don't regret it as Emily is doing really well academically and is also mixing with a nice bunch of kids.
Rose from London, mum to Emily, seven

We visited three schools locally, even though we knew we wanted the Catholic primary for our twin sons. It was very apparent that the Catholic and Church of England schools in our area had much stronger moral values than the non-faith school, and also got much better Ofsted inspection scores and test results. If we hadn't got a place at the Catholic school we'd have been happy with the C of E, but not the secular.
Arianna from Harrogate, mum to Dimitri and George, five

We have three primaries within walking distance: one only takes 30 children (so there's a chance we won't get in); one won't offer us a place because we don't worship; and one is awful. We started looking at schools we would be happy to send our son to that were further away but the council's admissions team was very disparaging about this approach. Apparently it's best to list the ones you are most likely to get into. But what if you don't want your child to go there? I went to see five schools in all and I found a lot of differences. Much hinged on the energy of the head teacher but some of it was a gut feeling. There's not much time to really get a sense of how the school operates in a one-hour visit.
Vicki from Bromley, mum to Ethan, four

I have always favoured Catholic primary schools and know they tend to be popular. I got my son christened within a Catholic church, so I hope this helps him to get a place. I believe in good education and religious morals. I have strong family values and would like him to learn about God.
Alicia from London, mum to Kyrus, four, Demiya, two, and Romareo, one

The school closest to our home has always had a pretty bad reputation, so my husband and I only really visited it as a formality. But when we met the staff and the new head teacher, who had only been in place for two terms, we were so impressed. The feel of the place was warm and welcoming; there were whole walls covered with displays of the children's work; new equipment had been installed in the classrooms and gym; and the head teacher's speech was really encouraging. We both thought the school had all the right potential and the fact that we'd be able to walk both

> ways was the icing on the cake. Grace had two friends applying to the same school, too, so she was really excited at the thought of going there. When we got the offer letter we had a small family celebration!
> *Elaine from Manchester, mum to Grace, four*

Make sure you go there

You won't be able to make a good assessment of what schools are like and whether your child will fit into them unless you actually go there for yourself and see how it feels. Visit all the schools in your area if it's practicable: sometimes getting a real feel for the place and seeing facilities and the classroom setting at first hand is worth more than all the other criteria on paper. In any case, you should certainly visit any schools you're seriously considering applying to.

Schools will often advertise open days or evenings when any prospective family can come and meet the staff, look at the facilities and ask any questions they may have – you can find out when these are going to take place by contacting the school direct, or checking its website. Many schools will be very happy for you to come at any time, though, and will make an appointment for you to do so – although they're very likely to ask you to avoid coming during hectic times such as registration or lunch.

When you're in a school, you should be able to 'feel the vibe' and get a sense of whether or not the environment will suit your child's personality. Indications that it's a happy place to be should be all around you: do you get a welcoming feeling? Is there work displayed on the walls, or are any reward schemes in evidence? Do the pupils look happy and engaged, and the teachers seem lively and interested? Be sure to use the opportunity to ask lots of questions. There's a list of specific things you might want to ask in Appendix II at the back of the book.

If they're invited, take your little one with you when you go to visit a school. It will mean it's not a completely strange place to them when the time comes to start, if they do end up as a pupil there. For the same reason, it's a great idea to go to the school informally if the chance arises – for instance, attending fêtes or car boot sales.

> ***Emma says:*** Your knowledge of how your child likes to learn, if they need any additional support, of any special interests they have and what really motivates them, will help you to decide if a school is suitable for them, too. Before you visit any schools think about what you want for your child and what type of environment would suit him. Go back for a second visit if you think that you need to find out a little more information. Don't forget to ask about after-school activities and clubs if this is something that you think your child will enjoy.

The application process

You will need to apply for a primary school place at a time dictated by the admissions timescale set out by your local authority (who co-ordinate the admissions process for all types of state school, even if they are not the admission authority for them). Information and application packs for school admissions are made available in the autumn of the school year before your child is due to be eligible to start school (for more on school starting age, see page 20). You may have one of these already: if you've registered an interest with a school, they might send you one, or you may get one through your pre-school provider. Don't sit back and assume one will plop through the door, though – it has been known for parents to miss the applications deadline because they didn't realise the onus was on them to apply.

Contact your local authority's school admissions team to check on their admissions schedule if you're unsure when and how to get an application form.

You'll need to complete an application form online or by hand. Some parents prefer to hand-deliver theirs, safe in the knowledge that it's definitely reached the right person, or because they don't quite trust the online system. However, if you do apply online you'll get an emailed acknowledgement and special reference number, which allows you to track it, update and/or otherwise change it right up to the closing date. After this time, you can still view your application, and you may be able to find out the result more quickly than if you have to wait for a postal offer, so it's certainly worth considering.

Do list as many preferences as you can on your application and make sure there's at least one acceptable alternative to your number one choice, which your child has a good chance of getting into. Only listing one or two schools won't increase your chances and if you don't get a place but haven't put an acceptable alternative down, you could be allocated something you really don't want.

Make sure you know what the deadline is, and that you don't miss it! If for some reason you do, you can still apply – it's known as applying outside the normal admissions round – but you'll be placed beneath all the applicants who *did* make it on time and that means you're unlikely to get a place at a popular school. (You won't be penalised further, though: if you then go on a waiting list, you'll be no further away from the top of it than the punctual parents.)

Depending on your LA's admissions schedule, you should get a decision some time between March and May. You'll be given a deadline by which they must have received your reply slip indicating whether or not you wish to accept the place offered.

What the Netmums say

How did you find the application process?

I applied online and it was so straightforward but I must admit I was terrified that it hadn't worked, especially around the time when the allocations were released! I applied online again this year for my youngest. The most stressful thing was the waiting time. Both applications were made at the beginning of September and we had to wait until the following Easter to find out which school they got.
Aimee from Chester, mum to Lauren and Megan, five, and Sophie, three

It was simple. We only visited one school as I was very sure my daughter would be offered a place there. I checked Ofsted reports and league tables and was lucky enough to know some parents whose children were already there, and I had a family member who taught on supply, so I had a couple of different opinions on the school and was happy.
Yasmeen from Birmingham, mum to Laila, four, and Sofia, one

I found the whole school application process very stressful as I really wanted to get the children into my school of choice. It was the talk of the nursery mums for a few months and, however hard you tried to not think about it, you couldn't help it. We visited two schools and they were very different! One was large and had better facilities, and the other was small and had more of a community where staff knew every pupil and parental involvement was welcomed. I went for the latter and couldn't be happier.
Lucy from Dunblane, mum to Archie, six, and Dugald, four

If you don't get the place you were hoping for

Try not to panic if you don't get a place at a school you're happy with. It's understandable that you'll feel upset, angry and worried but, at this stage, you'd be wise to try and be as positive and philosophical as possible. After all, only a third of parents win a school admissions appeal, so it's quite possible the place you've been allocated is the place you'll end up taking.

Try not to be too negative about the situation, particularly in front of your child – otherwise you'll have a lot of smoothing over to do if and when he has to start at the school you've been complaining bitterly about. Get some good advice as soon as possible – the best port of call at this time is ACE, the Advisory Centre for Education: they have a freephone advice line and a website full of detailed information about what you can do, including step-by-step guidance on how to appeal a decision (see page 196).

Before you do anything else, though, it's worth putting your name on the waiting list of the school you've lost out on, or indeed any you'd be happy with, since any places that become available (because other parents have turned down offers, moved, or even decided to go private or to home educate) must be filled from this list. You'll be ranked on the waiting list in the same order as the school's oversubscription criteria – priority isn't given according to *when* a name was added to the list. However, the school should be able to tell you where you are on the list and if you've got a realistic chance of getting in. Don't be put off by the fact that the list seems long and don't be complacent if you're near the top: it's quite possible to be moved up or down it.

It's also a good idea to reconsider alternative schools, even if they weren't on your original list, and find out if they have places. (It may well be that once your child has taken up an alternative school place and settled there, you won't want to move them, even if a place at your preferred school does become available: friendships are forged;

relationships with teachers have developed; the child feels comfortable and familiar with the school and its routine; and it would prove more disruptive than beneficial to move him.)

Of course, if you're truly unhappy and very determined to win the place you really want, then it's your right to lodge an appeal.

Dr Bob says: At the end of the day, you may not be able to obtain a place for your child at the first school of your choice. The most important thing here is to do all you can not to convey your distress to your child. Few things are likely to be more damaging to even a young child's progress than the feeling that they are about to attend a second-rate school. One of the most influential factors in improving school performance and external rating is the support of the parent body. You can play a very significant part in helping to bring about such change by conveying positive messages to your child about the school and by offering to become involved in any voluntary activities that the school may provide.

Appealing the decision

Again, things may vary from one admissions authority to another. The procedure for appealing if you don't get a school place that you're happy with – or if you don't get a place at all – will have been detailed in the letter outlining your offer. It should also give you a deadline for appeals. In some areas you can appeal online but more usually you will be called before an independent panel of around three to five adults. Your appeal can only be about one school at a time, so if you are appealing about more than one, you must attend an appeal hearing for each.

Bear in mind that if the school you are appealing about has already reached its legal limit for the number of pupils in each class – the legal maximum for an infant class is 30 – your appeal has very little chance of success unless it's found that the admission arrangements were not properly implemented; the arrangements are found to have been contrary to criteria set out in the School Admissions Code; or the decision is found to be unreasonable.

If your appeal is to be heard, you'll get at least ten days' notice beforehand and your appeal has to be heard within 40 school days of being lodged or before the end of the summer term, if that falls sooner (or within 30 days if your application was made outside the normal admissions process). A representative of the admissions authority will be present at the appeal hearing, who will explain to the panel why your application was unsuccessful. The panel will then ascertain whether or not the school has abided by the mandatory requirements of the School Admissions Code, and if these requirements have been applied correctly in the case of your application. If the panel can find no reason to overturn the decision from these initial investigations, you'll get an opportunity to make your case: explaining why you believe the school offers the best opportunities for your child; explaining any special circumstances you feel should be considered; and supplying any relevant documentation, such as evidence of a special medical or social need.

Your child will be offered a place only if the appeals panel decides that your case is stronger than the school's case against you. You will know whether or not you have been successful within seven days of the hearing. The decision of the panel is final and can only be overturned by the courts.

In the meantime, you're best advised to take up whatever school place you have been offered: this won't compromise your appeal or any further appeals you may make, and it won't affect your place on your preferred school's waiting list either. You're required to provide your child with an education, once they're of statutory school age (see page 20), so if you're determined not to put them in school while the appeal process is taking place, you may want to consider home education. There are links to some useful organisations in the appendix if you want to find out more about this.

What the netmums say

What happened when you didn't get in?

I was very disappointed when Ellen didn't get a place at our preferred primary school, having attended the nursery there. She was confused and upset about why she wasn't 'allowed' to go there when her friends had been given places, and it took her longer to settle into Reception at a new school with a whole new group of children than I think it would have otherwise. We're happy enough now, but I'd still have preferred her to have had a less traumatic start to school life.
Hannah from Stockport, mum to Ellen, five

My son did not get into his first choice of school, which I chose purely on the basis of its Ofsted report. He was one of 127 children applying for just 30 places. After he was refused I visited the second-choice school. I found a cosy, friendly school that the parents and children said they loved and discovered two of my friends were sending their children there because of its good reputation. I visited the first-choice school later in the day to hand in a form keeping him on the continuing interest list. I found a cold-looking, formal school with unfriendly snotty staff and even a mum with bad manners. So instead of handing in my form, I told them I had accepted my second choice!
Sally from Leeds, mum to Kye, four, and Lottiemay, one

> We didn't get our first-choice school for our son, we got our second choice instead. We did go to appeal and failed. I'm still very upset about the whole thing, but trying not to rub my negativity on my son, as he seems happy about the new school. My problem mainly is the distance. Also, there's no nursery so my daughter will have to go to a nursery near home and I've no idea how I can be in two totally different places at the same time at some point in the day, especially as I don't drive. I'm very disappointed in the whole system.
> *Michelle from Woking, mum to Craig, four, and Elise, one*

What happens next?

Once you've returned your reply slip to the admissions authority, you might want to double check by phone they have received it. Then it's a case of sitting back and waiting to hear from the school. Usually you will be invited to an induction meeting, typically some time during the term before your child's due to start. These offer a great chance to have another look around the school, meet staff and ask questions (you could refer back to the list of questions in Appendix II that are tips on what to consider when you were looking for schools). Don't miss it!

3 Getting ready to start school

Time to prepare

During the months and weeks leading up to your child's start at school there'll be lots of things to do in terms of preparation, both practical and emotional, and it's a good idea to start getting ready with plenty of time to spare.

You don't have to take time off specially – in fact, a holiday right before the big day might just make your child more reluctant to leave you. But thinking ahead and beginning to prepare slowly and calmly will give both you and your child confidence that you're as ready as you'll ever be when the time comes.

Easing any worries

It's very normal for some children to fret in the run-up to their first days at school (while some may take it in their stride.) You can help ease anxiety by looking at some books together, relevant titles include:

I Am Too Absolutely Small for School by Lauren Child; *Starting School* by Janet Ahlberg; and *When an Elephant Comes to School* by Jan Ormerod.

Let your little one know that there's plenty of fun awaiting her. Acknowledge her feelings and empathise – you might say that you remember feeling nervous about starting school when you were little. In fact, you could recount some (happy) memories from your own school days and ask her what she's looking forward to: making new friends, or being a big girl in her uniform. Try to find out, gently, if she has any particular worries and talk these through in a low-key way. Let her know you'll be there for her if she needs you.

Make sure life stays on as even a keel as possible, too: now's not the time for disruptions like redecorating her bedroom or joining her up to new groups or activities. Be around for her and stick to your normal routine. She'll get comfort from familiarity.

Allow her to regress a little if she shows signs – it's a perfectly normal reaction to anxiety. She might want more of your time and attention, plenty of cuddles and a little bit of babying. Don't panic if she starts sucking her thumb or carting a long-discarded comforter around with her, and don't comment.

If she's become unsettled in the evenings or at night, that's to be expected, too. You might have to work at getting bedtimes back on track by using the sort of techniques that you may have relied on when she was a toddler: there's more on establishing good night-time and evening routines further down the chapter.

Keep up a positive, reassuring front, but avoid banging on about school constantly between now and the time of joining. If you do get the chance to point out some positives – if, for instance, a neighbour's child comes home with a fab-looking model they've made, or are excited from sports day – then be sure to 'big it up'. After all, this is an exciting time.

Emma says: If your child is especially anxious you could make a book about the new school. Speak to her soon-to-be teacher and see if they would take some photos of the classroom, the playground or where the children eat dinner. A nice touch would be to have her favourite teddy in each picture so that you can make a 'Teddy goes to school' book: that way all the different places will be familiar before the first day. Some schools may offer a home visit from your child's future teacher. This is a great way for the child to meet their teacher in an environment where they feel comfortable. When I have made home visits in the past I have taken a teddy for each of the children and asked if they will look after it until their first day and then bring it into school with them.

What the netmums say

What did you do to get ready to start school?

We read lots of books about starting school and role played schools a lot (this was easier when my oldest had started as she played a lot with her little sister and it really opened up talks about routines, what to expect, and so on). I also got simple alphabet sticker books and children's magazines to do with the girls and explained that they were a bit like school work: it really helped them to focus and start to enjoy doing some 'work' before school and be less scared of what that meant. I also talked positively about my own school days and showed them a photo of me at school!
Nicola from Edinburgh, mum to Hannah, eight, and Feena, six

Prior to my youngest daughter starting school we went up to the school a few times so that she could become familiar with

> how it looked. I also took her along at the start and the end of the school day so that she could see what happened. And I brought her a few books to read on starting school and used those to ask questions and for her to ask questions back.
> *Jeanette from Walsall, mum to Alexandra, 13, and Molly, five*

Induction meetings

At some point in the run-up to starting school – or possibly on the first day of school itself – you'll probably be invited to an induction or welcome meeting at the school. At this you'll learn what's expected of parents and pupils, and hear about various school policies and aims. And if you haven't got one already by then, you should get a school prospectus, which will contain loads of useful information (see page 27). There might also be an opportunity to buy bits of uniform, and perhaps to meet a representative from the PTA. Some schools will also use this meeting to outline the various ways in which literacy and numeracy are taught, and you might get some handouts outlining this to help you support learning at home. (There's more on this on page 168.)

Another benefit is the chance to meet some other parents and get a feel for who you might make a beeline for at the school gates. Children may or may not be invited along, but it's certainly a good idea for them to look around before they start, if they haven't already – there may well be a later induction session for them just before their official start date. In any case, it's a great idea to take them along to any events the school are holding over the summer so that it isn't an unfamiliar place on their first day.

Teaching skills for school

Primary schools (as well as many pre-school settings) prefer it if new joiners are able to accomplish basic skills with minimal help. These include: being able to go to the toilet (and letting you know they need to go) and wiping themselves and washing their hands; managing to eat with cutlery (if they are going to be having school dinners – there's more on this below); undressing and dressing themselves (a must before and after PE sessions); and holding a pencil and demonstrating a degree of hand-eye co-ordination. They'll expect some accidents, of course, and will give help if they need to, but you'll make the transition from home to school easier all round, and save her teachers work they could do without, if your child is practised in doing these basics for herself.

Her teacher will probably also appreciate some advance training in listening and communication skills, and some respect for discipline. There are other skills you can encourage before she starts, such as sharing and socialising with others; showing empathy; and taking part in discussions.

If you do need to teach your child any of these things, set your goals well ahead of time so you can take a relaxed approach and allow for a few false starts. If your child is clearly not ready, leave it a few weeks before trying again. Above all, don't panic: any anxiety on your part will transmit to your child and put her right off the whole process! And remember, even the brightest child may have difficulty in doing up buttons or recognising the need to go to the toilet – these are skills that rely on particular areas of brain development, which can occur at different rates in different children.

Lots of children start school having learned a few academic basics such as recognising letters or counting to ten, either through playing at home with you or as part of their early years learning. That's fine – but as a rule, you're better off not trying to get a head start on formal learning before they go to school. Not only is it best left to the professionals, who will probably have particular methods that you may not know about, but there's every chance they won't be ready and if that is the case, pushing them could actually set them back.

Coping with toilet issues

Once she's at school your little one will be expected to let teachers know when she needs to go to the loo, hold on a little while if need be, wipe her own bottom and wash her hands afterwards.

It might be an idea to try and get your child used to having to wait a little while to use the loo in the months preceding her start at school, since she may not be able to rush to relieve herself immediately when she is there, or she may have to wait in line to use it. If she asks to go during a meal, see if she can hold on until she's finished what she's eating; if you're out in the garden, make a pretence of having a quick task to finish before you can bring her indoors to the loo. Gradually extend the time until she can wait five minutes or so. If wiping and washing hands are not skills she's yet mastered, show her the way and give her plenty of time to get them sussed.

Do tell your child's teacher if there *are* any toilet issues. They'll be sympathetic (especially if special needs are involved), but they do need to know.

Self-dressing

Learning to get dressed is a pursuit that can leave you both in a tangle – of nerves *and* clothing. So make getting-dressed skills one of the things she learns in the run-up to school starting – but don't expect miracles. Some kids find it too confusing or time-consuming and would prefer you to do it for them, in which case try again at a later date when they're feeling a bit more independent. Others want to run before they can walk and end up with things on inside out, upside down or in a terrible tangle.

Try to remain calm and encouraging. If things go wrong, be positive – you might say something like, 'You've *almost* got it, but let me show you again.' Resist the urge to steam in and take over, unless your child wants you to do so.

If all else fails, remember that Reception teachers are accustomed to children who are wearing inside-out shirts, back-to-front sweaters and shoes on the wrong feet, after a PE lesson. She'll get there eventually . . .

Stress-free dressing

Choose easy fastenings

Zips and buttons are tricky for small fingers – Velcro and plastic poppers are a little simpler. Where possible, choose clothes without any fastenings at all, for instance, a sweatshirt rather than a cardigan.

Give her a head start

Lay all her clothes out on the bed for her in the order you want her to put them on, face down, so she'll be able to put them on the right way round first time.

Get no-fuss shoes

Go for shoes, professionally fitted if possible, with Velcro fastenings, rather than laces or buckles. Your child will enjoy the independence of being able to put her own shoes on. (Some kind of fastening is important to support the foot during this important growing phase when her bones are still hardening.)

Coat magic

You've heard of a hat trick, now here's a clever coat trick – lie the coat on your child's bed, inside up but upside down (i.e.

on its back with the hood/collar nearest to her). Spread the arms out to the sides and get her to slip her arms into them (even though it appears upside down still), then pull the coat up and backwards over her head. Hey presto – it's on the right way round and right side out!

Practising with PE kit
It might be worth having a few practice runs to help her become adept at putting on shorts, t-shirt and plimsolls (and taking them off again!).

Emma says: You can think up all sorts of incentives to motivate your child when it comes to getting dressed. We had a chart on the wall with pictures of clothes stuck to it. This helped my daughter select clothes in the correct order and made getting dressed a much easier task. As the time to start school got closer we practised changing into her PE kit and back again so that she wouldn't be confused when she had to do it in class.

Managing a pencil

The ability to wield a pencil and hold it steady enough to prepare to write is desirable, although less of a priority in primaries than toileting, feeding and dressing. Your child's teacher will very soon help her on her way with this task if she can't do it already when she joins the class. (And chances are she can – if she's been to pre-school or nursery, she'll almost certainly have been encouraged to pick up a pen there.)

If you're starting from scratch, begin with chunky crayons or (washable) felts, which don't need lots of pressure applied to produce a vibrant result. Once she's got the hang of that you could introduce chunky colouring pencils: she'll need a little more control to make an impression on the paper with these. Finally, bring in regular-sized pencils and let her try these – but don't take away the others just yet as she'll only get frustrated if the slimmer-line pencils don't work and she doesn't have an alternative.

Show her how to make a fist, then stretch out just her thumb and index finger. Place the pencil between her finger and thumb, with the barrel resting on her third, curled finger, and ask her to grip it. Get her to relax her fist until she has hold of the pencil comfortably: she should be holding the first third of the barrel rather than gripping it halfway or further along. Let her have a go at scribbling. If she finds the pencil keeps slipping out of her grasp, steady it for her by lightly holding the top.

Practise regularly with her until she gets more dexterous: it probably won't happen overnight and may take a few weeks. As with other skills, the key is to keep the pressure off but pile on lots of encouragement for any effort shown. So you might say, 'It's fantastic to see you holding that pencil like a big girl. You'll soon be able to make it colour properly!'

> ***Emma says:*** If your child is struggling with pencil control you could try lots of games that require her to pick up small objects, manipulate switches, twist jar lids, mould with play dough, pour liquid and scoop items using small spoons. All of these activities will help with co-ordination and hand strength.

Listening and communicating

One skill your little one is going to have to learn pretty quickly once she starts school is listening. Teachers need all ears and all eyes on them in the classroom and will soon have something to say about it if a child's attention is elsewhere. It's not a bad idea if she also understands the importance of doing as she's told.

Hopefully, you've always made a habit of talking regularly with her and stopping to hear whatever she's got to say back: it's the most important thing you can do to help develop her listening and communicating skills (as well as her speech and language). But if you make a conscious effort to step these things up in the months before school, it will really boost her ability to communicate in the classroom, and her teacher will thank you for it.

If she has a tendency to drift off, or to ignore you downright, now's the time to try and reverse the habit. When you need her attention, stop, get down to her level and speak clearly so she's in no doubt what you're looking for.

Do avoid statements like, 'You'll have to be good when you start school.' Tempting as such threats may be – you don't want the classroom to lose its appeal before she's even got there.

> ***Emma says:*** Mealtimes are a really good occasion to model good listening. Ask your child to tell you about something that she's enjoyed during the day and encourage her to listen to you and the rest of the family. You could ask questions to help her extend her descriptions and to show her that you have enjoyed hearing her speak.

Learning to enjoy books

Reading is one of the first skills your child will be taught, and reading at home will probably be the only homework she gets at first, so it's a great idea to instil an enjoyment of books as early on as possible. Your child may well be a fidget who doesn't like being read to; she may be slightly precocious in wanting to grab the book off you and be in charge of page turning; she may do better with board books or picture books where you can make up your own story or predict the outcome. Don't worry if the first books your child will entertain the idea of reading contain no words! The idea is to get her in the habit of enjoying books, while learning that we read from left to right and from the top of the page to the bottom – and the same applies to following a sequence of pictures.

Remember, you're not teaching your child to read – that's best left to her teachers, as their methods may well be different from yours. Your job is to engender an interest in and a love of books, if you can.

10 steps to book-sharing enjoyment

1 Find 10 minutes or so each day when you and your child can have uninterrupted book time.
2 Let her choose some books that look interesting: go to the library; pick up some bargains in supermarkets and discounted book retailers; or swap with friends and family.
3 First look at the front cover and chat to your child about what sort of book she thinks it is. Does it look funny? Cosy? Does it seem to be about animals? Is it colourful?
4 Have your child close to you as you read so that she can follow the pictures and/or text.
5 Talk about the story during and afterwards, but if you're breaking off from reading make this clear to your child, then let her know when you've started reading from the book again.
6 Ask her to point at the pictures and repeat the words as you say them: 'Find the duck. That's right – that's the duck'; 'Where's the farmer? Yes, there's the farmer.'

7 If she can recognise her own initials, get her to find them among the text. She might only recognise them as capital letters at this stage; take your lead from her so you don't confuse her.
8 Ask her to predict what the next word in a sentence will be, using the pictures as a guide. For example, say: 'The farmer took the egg out from underneath the warm feathers of the . . . ?' If she says 'hen', point to the word and give her lots of encouragement for getting it right. If she gets it wrong, praise her attempt and simply say the correct word, avoiding the temptation to mock, even in fun. (It would be very easy to say something like, 'When was the last time you heard of a pig laying an egg?!' or similar, but this might result in a reluctance on her part to play the guessing game.)
9 Talk about the story after you've finished – but only if she has enough concentration left. If not, put it to one side to read it again soon. That way you can ask her what she remembers about the book before you begin next time.
10 Don't worry if she seems interested in only one book for now. Make sure you have a supply of different titles, but again take your lead from her. Lots of children take comfort from familiarity and may show more enthusiasm for a book they already know and understand.

What the netmums say

Skills for starting school

One thing that I totally forgot about when preparing my little boy for school was making sure that he understood that there

would be no one to wipe his bottom for him when he went to the toilet: being an August-born child, he was a very young school joiner. Although he was perfectly capable of wiping his bottom himself, he always used to shout for Mummy to check and make sure it was clean. On his first couple of days he kept calling for the teacher to check it for him!
Helen from Peterborough, mum to Harvey, five

I didn't want to start our eldest off reading and writing before he began school in case I used a different method from the teachers, as this would probably have confused him. I did teach him to count, though, as I'm not sure how many different ways there are of doing that!
Lena from Norwich, mum to Lewis, six, and Callum, three

We knew that David was young for his age, so we didn't try to push too many new skills at once. My husband and I decided that feeding himself and being toilet trained were the priorities, so we concentrated on those. As far as we were concerned, he would learn pencil control and listening skills once he'd started school. He's getting on fine. I would say, don't put too much pressure on: they'll be under enough stress when they first start school and don't need pushing at home.
Elspeth from Huddersfield, mum to David, four

Sebastian hates getting himself dressed, but when I explained to him that a teacher or another child would have to help him if he hadn't managed it himself before he started at school, he suddenly found the enthusiasm to try. I think it was the threat of a peer – possibly even a girl – having to give him a hand that spurred him on. In less than a week he was doing

the majority of his own dressing, although he did get things back-to-front at first. We laughed it off together and I did it myself a few times, just to give the idea that anyone could make the same mistake!
Sally from Thetford, mum to Sebastian, five

When my son was at nursery, I started trying to get him a bit more independent by dressing himself. It used to take him ages, so I got a timer and used to set it for five minutes and say if he could get his clothes on before the timer went (just clothes, not shoes and socks – that was a whole other saga!) then he would get a reward. It worked really well.
Sarah from Woking, mum to Harry, five

Sasha really likes a set of mini pencils we found for her. They fitted her little fingers perfectly and, although they were as slim as regular pencils, the fact that they were short made them more controllable than full-length ones. She used to take them everywhere with a tiny notebook and 'write her diary' in lots of scribbles. We've still got them but she doesn't really use them so much now she can write properly and manage full-size pens. I think they were just special to that stage.
Jacinta from Bradford, mum to Sasha, five

Natasha and I used to make tiny 'books' together from when she was three. They would only be about eight pages long, with just a few words on each page. She felt so important giving the books their own titles and helping me staple the pages together that the content wasn't really important. I think one of them just said things like 'pink fluffy cloud' and 'silly brown bunny' on the pages, and Natasha added a little

squiggle in the appropriate colour. It does seem to have sparked her interest in books.
Helen from Harrow, mum to Natasha, five

My mum bought Sam some story tapes for bedtime and he really did get better at listening. Up until then he wouldn't sit and listen to a story if I read to him, or watch a whole TV programme, but he loved the idea that a 'kind lady' would read him a bedtime story every night. There were sound effects, too, which he enjoyed and tried to copy. If I went in to speak to him during a story he'd say, 'Shhh, Mummy' and I had to wait until the tape had finished. They didn't help him to sleep much, mind you – he was much too engaged with the stories!
Deborah from Stoke, mum to Sam, five

A whole school day apart

If your child has spent whole days in a nursery setting before starting school, you'll both have the advantage of experience when it comes to coping with six hours or more spent apart. But for many mums and their children, a whole school day away from one another will be a new challenge. Even if your child has spent part-time hours away from you at a pre-school provider, a whole day at school is something different. And even if her school has a policy of part-time hours for newbies for a time to ease them in, then there'll be a full-day's separation to confront before too long.

If it's an experience she's not yet had, do provide some opportunities for your little one to spend a whole day away from you, preferably a good few times. Leave her first with someone she knows and loves well – grandparents, perhaps – and build up to a day spent with folk she's less familiar with (obviously you need to know and trust them). With no practice run at all of a life without you by her side, the wrench on that first day is likely to be a big one indeed.

Getting to know classmates

If your child already has buddies who are heading for the same school at the same time, then that's great: it makes such a difference to new starters if they can see a familiar face among their peers and it offers a sense of security and shared experience, which can make a lasting impression. So make the most of whatever friendships they already have with future classmates by getting them together for play dates beforehand.

If you know *of* other children, but don't know them or their parents particularly well, stick your neck out and issue an invitation anyway – chances are they'll be grateful for an opportunity to forge bonds before term starts. You could arrange to meet at a soft-play session or in a café with play facilities, if you're uncomfortable about inviting people you don't know well into your home. Once you're more comfy with each other and your children have bonded, too, you can start to swap play dates at home. Chatting over coffee while your children play can also be a great opportunity for mums to get to know one another.

If you don't know anyone at all, you can still get a head start on socialising – for you both – by asking the school to help you make contact with upcoming class members and their mums. Most schools will be happy to help, perhaps forwarding a letter from you or even providing contact details so you can get in touch. Often, someone will take the trouble to organise a large gathering during the summer preceding the new term – perhaps a picnic in the park – for anyone who's interested in coming along and getting to know some names and faces. Perhaps that organiser could be you?

What the netmums say

Making friends in advance

My daughter was very nervous about starting school. To help her I exchanged telephone numbers with another mum at one of the settling days before the summer holidays. During the summer holidays we met in the local park so the girls could play together. In the run-up to school starting, I reminded my daughter that she would see her friend on her first day. We also played 'schools' at home and got dressed, played, had a packed lunch together and talked about all the things she might do at school. This did help her settle very quickly and more happily.
Lisa from Caterham, mum to Abigail, five

I was so grateful to the mum who made contact with all the mums from the new intake and organised a big get-together in the park a month before school started. I met some really good friends that day – and so did Nina – which helped hugely when it came to overcoming those 'new school nerves'.
Julia from Milton Keynes, mum to Nina, seven, and Ellie, four

Practising the school run

It's a really good idea to familiarise yourself with the school run several times in advance of your child starting. Even if you're planning to walk there, get your child used to the route and the distance: it'll be one less 'strange' thing on this first day.

If you're planning to drive or take public transport to school, make the journey several times as if your child were already there: so leave at the time you think you will need to, and go back at the end of the school day, too. This way you'll discover how busy the route is; the frequency of buses/trains; any contingency travel arrangements; where to park, if you're taking the car; where any bottlenecks lie (and perhaps a few shortcuts to avoid them); and so on. There are few things more stressful than leaving in good time, then sitting in a traffic jam, watching the minutes tick by as you gradually edge towards being late for school.

Even if you're sure you've got the journey all sewn up well in advance of the school start, do run through it one more time during the week running up to the big day: you'll be able to check out whether there are any route diversions or road works that could hold you up, and your child will be familiarised with it one more time. (And remember that traffic is often very different in term-time, too.)

If your child wants to get to school on a bike or scooter, it's a good idea to give this a whirl beforehand, as well. But first, check your school's policy on bringing bikes and scooters on to the school premises (some schools ban their use within the grounds as they can prove hazardous to other people, especially if the 'driver' is a little wayward!). Make sure, too, that there's somewhere to store it where it will be protected and secure.

What the Netmums say

Trying out the school run

I found it useful to highlight some landmarks on the route to school. On the first day we played a game of guessing which one came next. This meant that my daughter was keen to keep moving and we arrived on time.

Amanda from Reading, mum to Kirsten, five

> We tried going on the bus a few times, then walking instead – it takes about 15 minutes. I couldn't believe it when Taylor actually wanted to walk, as she's only recently given up using a pushchair and has a tendency to be a bit lazy! I think it's all part of feeling more grown-up, although I shouldn't think she'll want to walk in the winter!
> *Esther from Ashford, mum to Taylor, four*

Getting the uniform sorted

While you won't want to splash out on your child's primary school uniform and school shoes until a short time before she starts (in case of a growth spurt which means they no longer fit), there are some items you could buy ahead of time to spread the cost, including suitable socks and perhaps new underwear; a school bag, if needed (lots of schools sell their own, sometimes with a logo on it); PE bag; a water bottle (many schools will ask you to provide one of these and make sure it's taken in, filled, every day – for more on that see page 98); and a lunchbox, if she'll be taking sandwiches. It's unlikely you'll be asked to get pencils or any other equipment, since these are almost always provided for your child in Reception.

Some schools have a strict uniform policy; others are more lax about what children can and cannot wear, and some schools don't have a uniform at all. You'll be able to find out what's required by asking the school for a comprehensive list or by checking the website or prospectus. If you've already attended an open or induction day/evening, a list may have been among the information given to you then – in fact, uniform or other bits like bags or hats may even have been up for sale at the time.

Typically, state primaries will stipulate the colour of the uniform but not the style – often with the exception of a sweatshirt or cardigan with the school logo on it – and allow you to purchase it from a supermarket or other affordable supplier. Even so, costs can add up, so hunt around for the best prices. Most manufacturers make school uniform items with practicality in mind anyway, but don't forget to look for non-iron items to make life easier on yourself. For instance, polo shirts, if acceptable, are a much better bet than cotton shirts with a collar and cuffs, because they take little or no effort to de-crease.

Some schools (especially private ones) have a set uniform only available from a dedicated supplier or from the school direct. If you find this prohibitively expensive, see if the school runs a second-hand uniform shop or stall.

What will they need?

You might be surprised at how quickly school uniform becomes dirty, so make sure you've got at least two of everything – and in the case of white shirts or polo shirts, three or four (many Netmums report that these tend to get filthy on a daily basis!). Two or three pairs of school trousers/shorts or skirts/pinafores, and two school jumpers or sweatshirts should be enough – it's pretty much vital to fork out for a spare for these items, not just because of laundry issues but because, at some point, one is very likely to go missing for a while! The same applies to ties for boys, if required.

A good pair of supportive school shoes, professionally fitted if possible, will be essential and, as young feet grow rapidly, it's a good idea to get them checked for size with every term that passes.

Summer dresses, if the option is available for girls, are a real boon: it's amazing the difference that putting on one item rather than two can make to your mornings! And even if you're looking at a September start, they can still work for the warmer autumn months with a cardigan and tights. If you're mum to a girl, you might want to check out the rules (or just general feelings) about hairbands and other accessories. It's often a requirement that long hair is tied up – certainly for PE days – and if your little lady wants to go in with sparkly pink bobbles or an elaborate (and expensive) hairband of some kind, you might have to persuade her otherwise.

Most schools won't issue specific rules about coats, but they might ask for them to be in dark colours, or request that they're showerproof and have a hood. (A packable mac is a good idea for warmer days when they don't need a coat but might get caught in the rain – in fact, some schools insist they always have some kind of jacket with them, just in case.) A hat, scarf and gloves are important for winter months, too, and – for the summer – a baseball or legionnaire's cap is essential. Most schools will make a point of prompting you about this when it's sunny. Hats that can be tied or buttoned on and gloves on strings that can be threaded through coat sleeves are also a good idea for younger children or those more prone to losing things. And they *will* lose things – that you can bet on!

If there's no uniform, it's a good idea to have a set of practical, hardwearing and inexpensive clothes that you set aside for school, anyway. That way you'll avoid morning arguments with a child who's dead set on wearing something inappropriate and you also won't risk nice, expensive things getting ruined when the going gets tough at playtime.

A little choice goes a long way

We all know it's tiresome taking children shopping with you, but it's a good idea to take yours when you go out to buy school uniform. Apart from the obvious practical issue of getting sizes right (uniform items often come up surprisingly large), most little ones find it an exciting experience and anything that puts a positive spin on a nerve-wracking event has got to be a good thing. Allow them some (but not too much) choice if you can: for instance, let your daughter decide between pinafores or skirts (or trousers, which are very commonly permitted for girls in schools now).

With shoes, you might have to lay down the law, because they will probably have to be plain black or brown and they should certainly be sensible. But most shoe shops offer a small choice of suitable styles, so if you can bear it, let her take her pick from an acceptable shortlist.

Emma says: Wearing school uniform is a very good way for your child to feel like part of the school community. It also saves arguments each morning about what your child wants to wear and avoids competition over who has the latest trainers, and so on. Many schools have a uniform supplier who will provide items carrying the school logo, but you may be able to combine these pieces with less expensive items from the high street.

The importance of labelling

It's a bind having to label every piece of clothing and equipment that will accompany your child to school, but unfortunately it's just about essential. When it all looks the same, young children will happily pick up and put on any piece of uniform, even if it isn't theirs, and it's astonishing how often a cardigan will get left in the middle of a playing field. Every school has an overflowing lost property box and chances are you'll be delving through it at some point. But you won't have much hope of putting a claim to anything that isn't named.

Thankfully, there's no need to sew labels in, since plenty of companies make iron-on tapes with your child's name at a very reasonable cost. Buy a really big batch to save time re-ordering later – you'll be needing them repeatedly over the course of her education. You can also get stick-on labels for use on hardware and shoe labels to stick inside school shoes, plimsolls and trainers. A cheaper option is to buy an indelible laundry marker pen and write on everything – blank labels are often provided in clothes or use the back of the washing instructions (not the front, otherwise you won't be able to read them).

Make sure you put your child's first and last names on everything: there may well be more than one child in school who shares your child's initials, or even with the same initial and surname.

Emma says: Labelling is absolutely essential! A teacher may have 30 children all wearing the same jumper and if they're not named it drives us mad. If your child is used to being called by a shortened version of his or her name (Alex for Alexander; Becky for Rebecca), it's best to use this to label his or her things. Some children don't readily recognise their long names, so if a teacher suddenly finds a drinking bottle labelled Robert So-and-So and its owner is more used to being called 'Bobby', it could result in some confusion!

Establishing new routines

Starting school is very likely to herald a whole new set of routines for your family, morning and evening (as well as after school). A good night's sleep and hence a nice early, calming bedtime will become essential (if it isn't already), and being able to get up and go first thing in the morning, five days a week, may be a challenge you haven't yet had to face (and one which leaves many parents defeated!)

Whether you need to establish whole new routines, or simply to tweak your existing ones so they're compatible with school life, make sure you start them early and get some practice in. Give yourself a good few weeks, and preferably a month, so you can make the adjustments gradually and fine tune them with time to spare.

Good nights

Research suggests that three- to five-year-olds need 10–12 hours sleep a night in order to function at full capacity, and children who are regularly sleep deprived can exhibit challenging behaviour, from irritability to emotional overreaction, poor concentration and even hyperactive tendencies. So you probably need to aim to get your little one to bed by around 7.30pm. If bedtimes are later than that at your house, you'd be wise to move them forward to a sensible time in the weeks leading up to the new term.

Just as when your child was a baby, the easiest way of altering a routine is to do it gradually, so you could bring her bedtime forward by ten minutes at a time over a period of weeks until you arrive at something you are happy with.

Happy mornings

Much as you may think your child will benefit from being left to lie in until the last possible minute on school mornings, she'll actually be better prepared for the day ahead – and separation from you – if she has a more gradual awakening. Try to allow a good 5–10 minutes just for her to become fully alert: wake her gently, sit with her for a bit, let her have a good stretch and tell you about any dreams she remembers. Starting the day with a sense of panic will just stress you all out.

You'll no doubt develop your own schedule in the morning but, as a general rule, make sure you have *at least* an hour to get up and ready – some families need an hour and a half, others two. And don't forget to give yourself time to get ready as well – although, if you can do as much of this as possible before attending to your little one, you can concentrate on her needs and there'll be less stress all round. In time she'll be more self-sufficient at things like getting dressed, teeth cleaning and hair brushing, and you'll have a bit more freedom to concentrate on your own clothes and grooming!

What your morning routine might be

- Wake her up with a kiss or cuddle and, when she's ready, a brief chat. If she has a stereo in her room, a little quiet music can help her come to – or you might choose to have a radio on elsewhere.
- Encourage her to go to the bathroom, use the loo, have a hands-and-face wash and clean her teeth. (Dentists recommend brushing before meals to remove plaque to which sugars and foodstuffs can adhere.)
- Let her choose and help make breakfast. (There's more on breakfasts below.) Help her dress if she can't do that by herself (many stubborn little ones will be determined to try anyway, which can be frustrating if time's short. You're probably better off taking a deep breath and letting her get on with it rather than insisting on taking over, which could cause tears or tantrums, and make you even later in the long run).
- Make sure hair is brushed – boys too – and put long tresses into neat plaits or a pony tail.
- Now would be a good time for her to do a poo, if that's usual for her at this time of day, so she starts the day feeling comfortable (and particularly if she prefers to do her poos at home, rather than at school). Give her plenty of time to do so without stress.
- Double check she's got what she needs for the day in terms of books, kit and outer wear (you'll very soon discover that doing as much as possible to prepare this lot the night before is your best bet – there's more about this on page 127). You'll probably have your own checklist, too – keys, handbag, umbrella, shopping list?
- Help her put her shoes and coat on. (This is where you

realise it was a good idea to practise these skills with plenty of time to spare!)

- Always factor in an extra 15 minutes at the very least for things to go wrong, for instance a sudden need to visit the loo again; a missing glove; or tears over hair brushing – and for general dawdling purposes!

What the netmums say

Adjusting to new routines

It took a while to adjust the bedtime routine to fit in with my daughter's school routine, but at the start I just spent more time with her leading up to bedtime so that she wasn't upset. She's an early riser anyway so that was OK, but she did have a few worries before bed (she is so much like her mummy!). I just talked them out then chatted with her and her teachers in the morning and they would give her a cuddle and reassure her.

Tara from Havant, mum to Morgan, six, Amy, three, and twins Emma and Jessica, one

Because they'd been at the college nursery for the year before school, both my girls were used to very early mornings. We actually get up later now that they are in school: we used to leave at 7.45am but now we leave almost an hour later! I'm slightly stricter than I used to be at bedtime. They used to be in bed by 7pm and asleep by 7.15–7.30pm; now they are in bed at 6.45pm and asleep by 7pm. Just those extra few minutes really help!

Aimee from Chester, mum to Lauren and Megan, five, and Sophie, three

Emma says: You could try using a visual timetable to motivate your child in the mornings. Take pictures of your child engaging in each of the activities in your morning routine and put them on a shelf in the order they need to be completed. Each time your child completes one task, remove the picture. Once all the pictures have been removed she could receive a sticker on a chart or some other small reward.

Brilliant breakfasts

Breakfast is *really* important for schoolchildren. A good nutritious start to the day will give your child the energy she needs to make it through the morning and, in fact, studies have shown that regular breakfast consumption results in children actually concentrating and performing better at school. Scientists even believe a good breakfast can boost feelings of wellbeing and make you happier! So whatever you do, and however late you may be, don't be tempted to skip it on a school morning. Hopefully you've already got some good breakfast habits in place but, if you haven't, now is a good time to start.

When it comes to breakfast, try to avoid sugary foods and go for things that release energy slowly, known as low-GI (glycaemic index) foods. Examples are wholemeal, wholegrain and wholewheat breads and cereals, porridge oats and fruit, especially dried fruit and berries. Other good nutritious breakfast options are eggs, mushrooms, yoghurts and peanut butter. Offer a drink in the form of milk, water, or fruit juice, preferably diluted.

Obviously you need something that's quick to prepare because time's always short in the mornings – fortunately, you can't go far wrong with wholemeal bread and butter or a bowl of healthy cereal. Don't let lack of time put you off offering a hot option sometimes, though, especially on cold days. Porridge is undoubtedly one of the best ways to start the day and is generally very popular. It can be knocked up very speedily in a bowl in the microwave (from which it's also much more easily washed up than if you made it in a pan). Or how about a nice bit of wholemeal 'eggy' bread, which can be shallow fried in a little olive oil in a matter of minutes?

If you need more specific ideas, you could try offering: a toasted wholemeal muffin with Marmite; chopped up apple with yoghurt; a soft boiled egg and toast fingers; a bacon sandwich on wholemeal bread; toasted rye bread with spread and fruit jam; a blueberry muffin and a banana; or a fruit smoothie. There's lots more information and ideas on the food pages at Netmums.

Of course, your little one may be a creature of habit (and many are) and will want to stick with the same breakfast every day – as long as it's a reasonably nutritious one, it doesn't really matter. If you've got a fussy eater on your hands and she simply won't go for anything very much, remember that some breakfast is certainly better than none. So encourage her to eat whatever she chooses, within reason, before you set off.

School dinners or packed lunches?

You might want to give quite a bit of thought to this all-important question in the build-up to starting school. For some parents, it's a real boon if their child's eating a hot school meal in the middle of the day: perhaps because it takes the pressure off them to provide a second hot meal in the evening (which might be tricky if you work late or have got after-school commitments), or because they know that their child is more likely to eat a proper meal if she sees her peers doing the same. It can also be – whether you work or not – a real drag to prepare a lunchbox every day.

For other parents it will be important to provide a lunch themselves, so they know what their child has eaten – especially if they're not convinced by the quality of what's on offer in the canteen

– or if they prefer their child's main meal to take place at home with the family.

Opt for whichever fits in best with your routine and lifestyle, while allowing your little one – as far as possible – to have a choice in the matter, too. In most schools, there'll be the option of changing your mind at reasonably short notice. It's also quite usual to be able to have a combination of both: packed lunch some days, school dinner on others, in which case, it may be that some kind of compromise will work.

Choosing school dinners

If you're going to buy school meals, it's a good idea to familiarise yourself with the menu: some schools buy in lunches from outside caterers; some have their own staff who cook from scratch on the premises. Whether or not outside caterers are used has to do with the level of facilities the school can accommodate, utilise and maintain.

School meals have improved in recent years, thanks in part to Jamie Oliver, and all school caterers now have to meet certain nutritional standards by law, with a good balance of food groups, some fruit and veg always on offer, and limits imposed on the amount of junk food available. Even so, quality and standards vary, so if school meals are something you're considering, ask for a sample menu first and check to see that it's varied and seems to come in line with the requirements above. You might also want to find out a bit about how lunchtimes work: are they staggered? In which case, will the younger ones get to eat first? Who is she likely to be sitting with? What will happen if she doesn't like something – will an alternative be found? And will supervisors check that she's eating her meal and let you know if she's regularly not?

If your child has any food allergies or any other specific needs, check whether or not these are fully catered for. And don't forget to find out whether water is readily available to drink at mealtimes (there's more on drinking water in schools on page 98).

There's lots more information which will help you make an informed decision about school dinners on the Soil Association's *Food for Life* website, and at the School Food Trust (see page 198).

If you do opt for school dinners, it's important your child can manage cutlery by herself, so make sure you give her some guidance on how to do this well in advance. Perfectly good table manners aren't necessary (and probably aren't very likely, either) but basic skills like holding her knife and fork in the right hand and cutting food are – lunchtime supervisors won't be offering this service to her.

Collecting her own food on a tray is very normal practice in school canteens and getting it back to the table in one piece without dropping it is likely to be a challenge – losing her lunch on the floor is definitely not something you'll want, especially as there may not be a complete replacement available, since school canteens tend to work to tight numbers (one mum was horrified to hear her little one had to survive on a bread roll and an apple after her lunch went west one day). It might be worth a few trial runs with a tray at home.

Free school meals

Your child may be eligible to get free school meals if you or your partner receive certain benefits. The free school meals policy only applies in England and Wales and is usually run by the education department of your local authority or governing bodies in your area.

In Scotland, free school meals are at the discretion of the Scottish Government and criteria can be found on its website.

Choosing packed lunches

If you're going to provide a packed lunch for your child, try to make sure it offers a fairly healthy balance of foods – there's more on how to do this below. Sending her lunch to school with her gives you an ideal opportunity to encourage her to eat healthily, as she's more likely to eat what she's given than go hungry.

Try to avoid crisps, chocolate bars and other high-salt, high-fat or high-sugar foods from the start – or at the very least make them very occasional treats – so she comes to accept that her lunchbox is a healthy zone. If you put these things in regularly she'll soon start to expect them every day – or, worse, eat only the unhealthier parts of her lunch and leave the rest.

Don't forget to include a drink: water's your best bet (if you're planning on including juice or squash, bear in mind that some schools will prefer you not to as they're sticky and less healthy, while fizzy drinks are very often banned outright – so check the rules or guidelines first). In fact, all children should be drinking water throughout the school day to keep themselves well hydrated (see page 98).

Make sure your child can manage all the fixings on her lunchbox and any other containers, and provide a sports-type, non-spill bottle with a secure lid for her drink: leaking drinks are a well-known annoyance for school staff as they ruin bags and books and require mopping up. Add in a piece of kitchen towel for her to wipe her hands on.

Be sure to check out any rules about school lunches (or, if not rules, there may be guidelines which you are asked politely to abide by). If you are asked not to bring chocolate or foods containing nuts in to school, always co-operate because of the sensitivity of some children to nuts and nut products, and the possibility of food sharing at lunchtime (even if it's against the school rules). In any case, there are plenty of healthy alternatives, and if one parent seems to be getting away with flouting the rules, the school will soon have an uprising on its hands.

What to put in a lunchbox

When you're packing a lunchbox, try to include a combination of some starchy carbs, some protein, a bit of dairy and some fruit and/or veg. Good carb/protein combos are rolls or sandwiches filled with tuna, cheese, ham, chicken, hummus, Marmite or egg. And don't forget you can experiment with different sorts of breads sometimes for variety, including chapattis, pitta bread, tortilla wraps, bagels or muffins – although, as with breakfast, you may find your little one prefers to stick with what she knows and may balk if she opens her lunchbox to find something new. Add a bit of salad as the fruit/veg component, such as tomato, lettuce or cucumber in sarnies, or serve separately in the form of crudités, perhaps with a little pot of soft cheese (which also covers you on the dairy front) or guacamole (which will count as a portion of veg) to dip them in.

Pasta or rice salad with added cheese, ham, tuna, shredded chicken, vegetables or beans makes a healthy alternative to a sandwich. You could also consider serving proteins separately, for instance a chicken leg, cold sausage, mini cheese or hard-boiled egg (although she might get teased for the smell of this), perhaps with a buttered roll on the side providing the carbs. That way you avoid the problem of sandwiches made soggy by their fillings.

For dairy, you can't go far wrong with a bit of fromage frais or yoghurt, with cheese a good alternative. And for fruit, a single, small piece of fruit, pot of fruit salad, or box of dried fruit are all good offerings – lots of children prefer their fruit and veg peeled and sliced or diced, so do this if it means she'll eat it, but bear in mind it might go dry or brown, which may not be very appealing.

Add in a healthy-ish treat sometimes. You can bet your boots that however hard you're trying to keep junk out of his box, there'll be other children tucking into crisps and cakes on a daily basis and, while that shouldn't be a reason to drop your own standards, it can be tough on the child who has to go without. Make sure your treats have some nutritional value as well and it won't matter so much: an oaty biscuit; a piece of buttered malt loaf; a homemade muffin or carrot cake; or a little tub of popcorn are all good examples.

From a health point of view, it will be so much better if you make your child's packed lunch from scratch – pre-packed sandwiches, pies, or other convenience foods tend to be loaded with salt and other additives she could do without. If you don't have much choice but to pack these things sometimes, because you're short of time, try and do so infrequently – or consider swapping to school dinners, which will almost certainly be a healthier option than a packed lunch consisting of pre-packed products.

One final word of caution: don't assume that your child is definitely eating everything in her lunchbox just because it's empty when she gets home. There may be surreptitious opportunities for her to slide unwanted items into the bin, or she may have offloaded it on to a less discerning lunch companion. Equally, it's quite possible she will have consumed something you'd rather she didn't, if someone has been kind enough to share the contents of their lunchbox. You'll never be able to retain control of this situation entirely, but you could have a word with a teacher or lunchtime supervisor, if you're concerned it's happening, and ask them to keep an eye out.

You shouldn't need to pack a snack, as Reception children receive a free piece of daily fruit or veg as part of a government initiative. If your little one turns her nose up at fruit and you want to provide an alternative, check with the school about their rules on that: they're very likely to request that you make sure it's a healthy one.

What the netmums say

What's for lunch, mum?

Laila usually has school dinners two days a week and packed lunches the other three. I chose to do both as I want to be able to see what she eats in her packed lunches but I also want her to experience school dinners so that if, for example, I can't do a packed lunch one day, she won't freak out. She's actually asked to have school dinners all next week, so they must be doing something right!
Yasmeen from Birmingham, mum to Laila, four, and Sofia, one

My kids prefer packed lunches as every day is like a mini picnic for them. It means I know what they've eaten and can vary it daily to fit in around their activities, so if they have an after-school club I'll give them more food because there's an extra hour to wait until home time; if they have swimming or PE at school I give them high-energy foods like bananas, and so on. I also feel that if my children ate a full cooked meal at school they wouldn't want to have another at teatime – and teatime is a major part of our family time as everyone sits together and talks about their day.
Laura from Rutland, mum to Malachi, seven, Cian, five, and Kerenza, three

Nina hates the whole idea of eating off those plastic plates and having to try a stranger's cooking. She's also aware that dinnertime supervisors at her school patrol the dining room encouraging children to clear their plates. All in all, packed lunches are the right choice for her. Also, as she's a bit of a grazer, she often saves things up to have on the way home from school. She's better with small amounts of food more often rather than a big meal three times a day.
Rochelle from Watford, mum to Nina, five

Matthew is a much better eater since he started having school dinners. It's probably because he tends to follow other children's lead and all his friends prefer a proper meal to sandwiches. I'm not completely happy with the menu the school offers, but I'm more concerned that he wants to eat full meals at all. Before he started school he was much happier to eat lots of small snacks instead.
Dominique from Telford, mum to Matthew, five

I gave Nina packed lunches when she started school, because she's so fussy I feared she wouldn't eat anything served up in the canteen. I hated making a box for her in the mornings, though, as it was so much hassle. Then one day she requested I put her down for a school meal on 'fun Friday', the day they serve chips! Then it was Wednesdays, which is roast day. Now she has school dinners five days a week. What a result. I'm happy because I know they're pretty good quality and I can worry less if she's picky over her evening meal. I must say, I suspect she's eating things at school which she refuses to touch at home. I can live with that!
Julia from Milton Keynes, mum to Nina, seven, and Ellie, four

Keeping them well watered

Drinks aren't just important at lunchtime: all children should have the chance to drink water throughout the day because studies have shown that staying well hydrated boosts concentration and good behaviour, as well as health and wellbeing generally.

Although not a requirement by law, most schools these days are well tuned in to the benefits of water and there should be a fountain or dispenser for your child to drink from, either freely, at breaks, or with permission during class time, or you may be asked to provide a water bottle. Remembering to fill it, pack it, and empty it daily (always assuming she has remembered to bring it home!) is likely to become one of the many things on your school prep to-do list, but it's an important one.

A good tip for the summer is to fill the water bottle to three-quarters and then freeze it: it will start to thaw on the way to school and remain cool throughout the day (and if you pack it in with her lunch, if she takes one in, it will keep that cool, too).

There's more on the benefits of water on the website of the Water is Cool in School campaign (see page 197).

4 What starting school means for *you*

A big deal for mums, too

Let's face it, if this is the first time you've seen a child off to school, it's going to be quite a wrench. If you've been at home with him until now, you'll have got used to being in each other's company for hours at a time and may feel more than a little bereft at the prospect of being without each other. But even if you're a working mum and accustomed to separation, don't underestimate the emotional impact of your child starting out in the big world of school life. You've still got to watch him put that uniform on for the first time and wave him through those great big school gates. And chances are that as a working mum you'll have a few guilt issues to contend with, too, because you know you won't be there on every drop-off, and there'll probably be assemblies and other events, over time, that you're going to miss.

That's just the emotional issues – you've undoubtedly got some practical ones, as well. What you are going to do for childcare, for instance, or what you're going to do with yourself. Childcare arrangements, in particular, are going to be top of your to-do list, and it's really important to get them right: if your child is uncertain or unhappy about who's looking after him and when, it's likely to make the settling process a whole lot harder.

Whatever you're looking at in the way of new arrangements, be sure to give yourself loads of time to get them in place before the new term – or wait for a good bit of time afterwards, and do it when the dust of starting school has settled.

So what next?

If you've been a full-time mum and this is your only child, perhaps you're wondering how you're going to fill your time. A return to work, full- or part-time, is very likely to be a consideration. Or if money's not a pressing issue, maybe you're going to throw yourself into some home improvements or start some voluntary work (and, if so, perhaps you'll investigate the possibility of helping at the school itself – there's more on that on page 158).

If you're a working mum already and have childcare arrangements in place, perhaps things won't change that much – but there may still be some adjustments to be made. For instance, if your working hours go beyond school ones, you'll need to sort out someone to do the school run, one or both ways. It may be that you or your other half can alter your working hours, with a later start or earlier finish time, which will allow you to drop off or pick up. Or maybe this will be a good time to look at a change of career entirely, swapping it for one that fits better with school hours.

Perhaps you also have a younger child or children and you've no plans other than to be at home with them right now. The extra time you'll be able to spend with them will be a great bonus – especially if, like plenty of parents, you've always felt a bit guilty about paying less time and attention to your second or subsequent babies. Your routine might not change too much, but the rush to get your child up and ready for school every morning, while dealing with one or more younger ones, can be a shock to the system. Mornings (and to a lesser extent, afternoons, when you've got to be at the school gates at the right time) are likely to be a considerable juggling act. Give yourself lots of time to get ready, do as much as you can in advance and remember – it will get easier the more practised you get at it.

Ditch the guilt

If you're a working mum, don't allow your child's start at school to fuel extra guilt because you're not around 100 per cent to ease him in. Do the best you can to sort out solid, reliable and consistent care outside school hours when it's needed, and spend as much 'quality' time as possible with him while at home and he'll be fine.

Working mums are contributing to family finances and that will be of benefit to your child. And working mums are good role models for their children, especially to their daughters. Not only that, but if you're someone whose career is a fulfilling and important part of your life, then you'll be a better parent if you're able to preserve your identity and self-esteem than if you sacrifice it to be at the school gates every day.

Getting the childcare you need

So, do you need to make whole new childcare arrangements – or are you going to be able to work with what you've got? That's likely to be the main question in your mind.

If you can continue to make use of the same care provider you had before then it's a bonus: it means your child won't have to go through the upheaval of getting to know someone new. For example, if he already attends a private nursery, you could find out if there's an option of fewer, flexible hours and, if so, if there's anyone you know who's willing and able to get your little one to school from there in the morning, and/or from school to nursery in the afternoon. Perhaps the nursery even offers drop-off and pick-up services (some do if the school is local – it's well worth checking). One major benefit of carrying on at a private nursery is that you can get care during school holiday time, too. It is, however, likely to be a pretty expensive option.

If your child's happily registered with a childminder, will this childminder be prepared to keep him for a shorter session outside school hours and, more to the point, to do the school run for you? Again, this will offer continuity but unfortunately there's every possibility that – if she's got other, younger children in her care, or she needs to do a school run of her own, in a different part of town – she won't be able to help.

Whatever existing form of childcare you've got going, it's worth taking a careful look and seeing if it can be adapted to suit your child's new schedule. If not, you're going to need to look for an alternative.

Finally, bear in mind that with a start at school you may well have to consider a hotchpotch of care provision. So maybe your mum picks up and takes home on Mondays and Tuesdays, your childminder has Wednesday to Thursday covered, and you manage to negotiate a 'work from home' day (see page 110) on Friday so you don't need anyone's help then. A consistent arrangement is always best, but as long as the arrangement stays more or less the same as term goes on, your little one won't be losing out.

Friends and family

Many parents ask a family member or good friend to step in when it comes to looking after their children outside school hours – after all, when it's just a matter of a few hours a day, many nans, granddads, aunties or other relatives are happy to help out. The great advantage is that it will be someone they know, who loves them. The main disadvantage is it may not be consistently reliable – you can't reasonably expect someone to offer 100 per cent commitment to caring for your child if you're not paying them the going rate and they have other stuff they need to do sometimes. And it might be that they're not so happy to help out for much longer periods come the school holidays – so you'll need to find out in advance how much cover they're prepared to offer. In any case, make sure all expectations are on the table before going ahead with an arrangement like this – try to find out what level of commitment they can offer, and make sure you know what they're expecting in return (don't assume it will be a free service – they might, quite reasonably, assume you'll be paying).

Lots of parents find some sort of reciprocal arrangement can work well: if you've got a good friend or neighbour with a child at the same school and you have different working hours which will allow for 'swapsies', for example, perhaps one of you could take and the other collect. Be careful who you make an agreement like this with, though: it needs to be someone you know, trust and like, pretty well – and that your child is happy to be with, too.

Relatively well cared for

- Treat any relative who's helping you with childcare as you would any paid-for childminder: let them know in advance if you want them to mind your child for longer so you can work late or go out; ring ahead if your journey has been disrupted; take into account that they have a life outside of minding your child!
- Offer to provide any food for your minder to give your child in the way of breakfasts or after-school snacks: it might work best if you drop off some shopping at the beginning of each week.

- By all means ask them to stick to any principles and boundaries that really matter to you, but don't be too precious about it. A couple of sweets here and there, or a bit more telly than you'd usually allow aren't going to hurt. Just make sure he's clear that 'granny's rules' don't apply at home.
- Air any concerns you may have straightaway rather than letting things fester, and check regularly that your minders are still happy with the set-up.
- Show your appreciation, even if they say it's a pleasure to look after your child. If you're not paying them in cash, give them flowers, wine, or vouchers sometimes – and make sure you return the favour however you can.

Childminder

Your best option for a childminder right now is probably one who's doing the school run already, with her own kids and/or someone else's in tow. This kind of detail won't necessarily be included in local authority lists of registered childcare providers, so you might need to use some nous and track one down for yourself. You could try asking around outside, or inside, the school – childminders are bound to be regular fixtures at the school gates and lots of people will know who they are, and perhaps even where they live or how you can get hold of one. Added to that, word-of-mouth recommendations are often the best way to hit upon someone you can trust. And finding a childminder who already has links with the school could be a definite plus: with any luck you'll get some good insider information, helpful hints and support, and maybe some introductions to other mums.

Once you've found a childminder who seems suitable, make sure you go through the same checks you would if you were asking her to look after your baby. (There's a good list of things to look for in a care provider on the Daycare Trust website and the National Childminding Association also has lots of info – see page 195.) For peace of mind, make sure she's registered so you know she's Ofsted inspected – this is certainly necessary if you're going to be claiming for financial help in paying her (see page 110). And find out how flexible she's prepared to be – can you pay her for just the few hours you'll be needing her? Will she charge you for an early or late arrival at either end of the day?

Bear in mind, too, that some childminders operate all year round and will expect payment during holiday times as well. Others operate during term times only – which won't be much use if you need cover during the school holidays as well.

Extended care services at school

Thanks to a government initiative that aims to get all schools offering some form of extended care either side of the main school day, more and more primary schools now offer this provision, either on the premises or nearby. Often known as extended hours services or 'wraparound care', this typically includes before-school sessions from as early as 7am, with breakfast provided, and after-school sessions that run until around 6pm. Waiting lists can be long, so it's advisable to make enquiries ahead of time.

School-based childcare will usually include a variety of supervised activities, which – if children of five and under are involved – must abide by the Early Years Foundation Stage framework (see page 4). They must be Ofsted registered (if open for more than two hours a day and catering for children under eight) and at least half the staff must have formal training.

This is another option that could work well as part of a patchwork arrangement, especially as this sort of provision is usually flexible and therefore available on a sessional or day-by-day basis. There's usually a fee to pay but, as they're subsidised, they're usually very affordable – generally anything from a few pounds to a tenner a session. (Don't forget you can claim help with this, if eligible, through Working Tax Credits. You might also be eligible for a free or reduced-rate place, depending on your circumstances. For details, go to Direct Gov, or check out the Daycare Trust's Paying for Childcare website.)

The great advantage of childcare within school is continuity and the comfort of familiarity for your child – there's no rushing to get somewhere else in between and he'll be in a place, with other children (and possibly some staff) he already knows. The downside is that he may be somewhat fed up with school after a full day there, and keen to just chill out in a home environment.

You can find out more about extended school services at the website of the Out of School Alliance and at the website 4Children (see page 195), or find out what's on offer and where in your area by contacting your local Families Information Service.

Holiday clubs and play schemes

Most working parents need at least some childcare cover in the holidays, too, and fortunately – as part of the same extended schools initiative that's boosted the number of after-school and breakfast clubs – there's now a good choice of holiday clubs and play schemes around. They're usually offered as part of a school's extended services but can also be run by private or voluntary organisations and may be held in schools, youth clubs, village halls and community centres. The average cost of a holiday club session is £20 per day, but it varies from area to area.

Nannies and au pairs

If you can afford it, the option of a nanny (or an au pair, if appropriate – see below) may be worth looking at once your child is school age because of the flexibility and reliability it can offer. It could even be cost effective if you've got more than one child, or if a nanny-share is an option – in other words, pooling the services of one nanny with another family and dividing the cost. Nannies may or may not live in the family home and will generally be more flexible and work for longer hours than a childminder.

If you employ a nanny, you'll be responsible for paying her tax and National Insurance contributions. You'll also need to check out her credentials yourself. Nannies don't need formal qualifications by law, but it's a good idea to look for some, or at the very least satisfactory references and plenty of experience. Neither do they have to be Ofsted registered – although they can voluntarily choose to be listed on Ofsted's Childcare Register, making some financial help in the form of Working Tax Credit or childcare vouchers a possibility.

An au pair will usually be an overseas student who's seeking to learn English as a foreign language and looking for a family to put her up. They're only really an option for parents with school-age kids, or kids who are also in some other form of childcare, since they're not required to have any formal childcare training, are not allowed to work for more than 25 hours in any week and cannot look after children under the age of two. They may, however, agree to babysit for two evenings a week outside these hours. An au pair could be a boon if what you mainly need is someone reliable to cover the school run and/or a short time either side of school. As well as the cost of their board and lodging, you'd need to give them 'pocket money' of between £50 and £70 a week. Another advantage in their favour is that they'll usually throw in some light cleaning and ironing duties, too.

Dr Bob says: Making the right childcare arrangements can have an enormous impact on how well your child settles at a new school. The child's immediate inclination is often to want to talk about their day, so if Mum can't be there to listen it's important that the chosen carer can empathise with the child and make him or her feel secure until Mum can be there. Under these circumstances, convenience may not necessarily be the most important criterion in making childcare arrangements. You need to put as much careful thought into this as into selecting the right school.

What the Netmums say

Juggling work, school and childcare

I work three mornings a week and, after asking around among my friends, I was able to find another mum who works afternoons on the same days. We live quite close to each other, so we've got an arrangement where she takes Abigail to school with her own daughter, Chloe, and I pick both of them up after school. We both have the remaining two days at home, so we generally take turns to do the school runs, depending on our commitments. It works out really well, and Abigail and Chloe have become great friends.

Nicky, mum to Abigail, five

It's been a mixed blessing using my mother-in-law as our main child carer. On the plus side, if my kids are unwell I'm happy knowing that I have left them in safe hands; the down side is that my in-laws take holidays in term time which means I have

to take days off, leaving me with little time off during school holidays, or having to take unpaid leave.
Jacqui from Swindon, mum to Sean, ten, Laura, seven and Daniel, five

My friend and I take it in turns to have each other's children after school: she works Tuesdays and Fridays, and I work Mondays and Wednesdays, so it works out really well. She only lives round the corner and our kids were friends from their nursery days so it's the next best thing to having our parents help, which isn't an option for me as both my parents and in-laws live abroad. For me, it's the perfect solution.
Kumu from London, mum to Naveed, five

Grace started school last September and things changed more than I had thought. My husband has had to request early morning shift work so he can pick her up from school but this is only a temporary fix as he's not able to do that forever. The school has a breakfast club that I use but sadly no after-school club. The real issue, though, is all the other things that go with school: Grace has quite a lot of homework every week that we struggle to do with her; the activities during the school day to which parents are invited often have to be missed, which Grace finds upsetting; I don't get to make friends at the school gate so Grace misses out on invitations to tea. Working to pay the mortgage and having children at primary school is far from easy.
Sarah from Witham, mum to Grace, five and Tom, two

I got a part-time job when Jamie started school, so I had to find a childminder. Luckily my mum-in-law was able to do the school run two days out of my three, and I've just found a childminder who doesn't mind having him just one day a

week, which is brilliant! There's another boy from his year who has the same childminder so it hasn't been too bad settling him. I think he finds the long days a bit much to cope with, but I'm sure he'll soon get used to it.
Adela from London, mum to Jamie, four

We've made great use of our school's after-school care service, which has really reasonable fees and provides exactly what we need – just an extra hour or so at the end of the school day because I don't finish work until five. The drawback, of course, is that they close in the holidays and then it's just a question of managing as best we can, with a combination of me and their dad taking time off, my mum helping out and several holiday clubs and play schemes. I've also got a couple of good friends who are willing to help, which is brilliant: I clock up as many 'favours' as I can by having their kids whenever I am around!
Alison from Reigate, mum to Max, nine, and Sophie, seven

Getting financial help with childcare

If you work, don't forget to see if you're eligible for financial help from the government in the form of Working Tax Credits or employer-supported childcare, which includes the childcare voucher scheme. The Daycare Trust's Paying for Childcare site is a great source of help and information on these things.

Options for flexible working

Chances are, if you work you've already explored your options for flexible working by now. But if not, perhaps this is the time to look into the possibility of reducing, adjusting, or compressing your hours, jobsharing, or working from home sometimes.

By law, if you are the parent of a child aged 16 or under and you have worked for your employer for 26 weeks, your employer must 'seriously consider' your request if you ask for a flexible working arrangement – and they have to give you good reason why, if they say 'no'. In other words, you have nothing to lose by asking. And this applies to everyone – so if it turns out you can't get more flexibility in your job, maybe your partner can. Or maybe you can both benefit.

If you are thinking about requesting flexible working, bear in mind it could take up to three months or more to get it sorted. Requests must be made in writing and you'll need to outline what sort of changes you're looking for, and when, and how it might affect things at work.

There are lots of useful sources of information on flexible working and the main ones are included in the back of the book. For more information about this, contact your local Citizens' Advice Bureau (CAB) or go to their online advice service instead. There's also lots of support and advice on offer from an organisation called Working Families (see page 198).

Being your own boss

Lots of mums find that a child starting school offers an ideal opportunity to set up their own business or take on a franchise, often providing a product or service that's family-oriented. The advantages of being self-employed are obvious – you set your own working hours, which means, in theory, you can be there for school pick-ups, sports days and assemblies if you need to. (Although it has to be said that if your business takes off you might find yourself as tied to your job as any ordinary working mum!) And if you are going to start a major project like this, you might want to wait until after you've got your little one settled – although there's no harm in starting your research ahead of time, so you're better prepared to get stuck in once you're truly free. There's tons of information and ideas about working for yourself and forums where you can chat to other mums who've done the same on the working pages at Netmums.

Another popular self-employment option for mums is childminding. As a registered childminder, you would need to offer care that abides by the EYFS (see page 4), make sure your home is suitable and be inspected by Ofsted. You might consider offering your services in term-time only, if that will suit you better, and you could also offer pick-up/drop-off services at your school, which is very likely to put you in demand.

For details of how to apply as a childminder and become registered, contact your local authority or check out the advice on the National Childminding Association's website.

What the netmums say

Making work more flexible

In a way, sorting childcare was harder when Jamie started school than when he was at nursery. When Jamie went to nursery at five months old, it was at times to suit us and our work, whereas now we have to fit round the school! I have arranged to finish work in time to collect Jamie and spend some quality time with him before bedtime – plus it means we can get homework done without having to rush it. Covering the school holidays is proving problematic and has only been solved so far by taking a month's leave without pay.
Ruth from Lancaster, mum to Jamie, four

My job as a civil servant in a benefits office fits in really well around my children, who are now both at school. When my eldest first went to school, I requested part-time/term-time

hours and got them. I work five hours per day, either 7am until 12pm or 10am until 3pm. My husband takes them to school before he goes to work and I pick them up. My job is great for people with families, as I get paid time off in emergencies, such as the schools closing due to the snow.
Lizzie from Preston, mum to Logan, seven, and George, five

When my first daughter was about 18 months old I tried to find a second job in addition to the dressmaking I was already doing. By chance I saw an ad for a Parish Clerk and to my amazement I got it. Other than one monthly meeting, I get to choose when I do my hours, so I can work at midnight in my PJs if I fancy it. I've even taken on a second parish. This means I can attend the myriad of school events, which is important to us because my husband's job means he is rarely able to get there. The downside is that I am neither a stay-at-home mum nor a working mum and, as such, I struggle to find my place in the playground. There are only a couple of other work-at-home mums and we tend to cling together for safety!
Lucy from Didcot, mum to Hope, five, and Elizabeth, one

I work 42 hours over a four-day week on a rolling programme. That means I work Monday to Thursday one week, then Tuesday to Friday the next, and so on. It also includes weekends. I'm lucky that I can nearly always manage to pick my daughter up after school so she can tell me about her day and what help she might need for the next day.
Vikki from Bradford, mum to Josie, four

Before he started school, my mum offered to have Nathan one day a week for me so I could do some voluntary work. I started helping out in one of the local charity shops – sorting

through donations and helping with window displays – but it was just the change I needed. I made a good friend there and when Nathan started school she encouraged me to apply for a paid role. Now I'm actually serving in the shop three days a week, 9am until 2pm, so it fits perfectly into school hours. I'm so glad to be back in employment, even though the money's not great. I feel I'm a much better mum for it.
Harriet from Redditch, mum to Nathan, six

My legal work for the police force used to begin at 9am and finish at 5pm, with on-call shifts at least once a week. When my daughter started school I found this hard because if I was in a police station I could not leave an interview to take her to school, so after ten years working on both sides of the fence (I used to be a Met Police Officer) I became self-employed. I now run two businesses. I do miss crime work more than I thought, but for the moment, I never miss any school activities, which I think is more important and I still get intellectual stimulus through work.
Clare from Lincoln, mum to Scarlett, five

When Harry was born, a senior position was open at my local nursery, so I applied and got the job. It was close to home and Harry went to the baby room from when he was four months old. We were there for four years and loved every minute. When my daughter Madison was born, I went back with her after nine months off and she didn't settle at all into nursery, so after six months we left and I started childminding from home. Now Harry is in school this suits us commitment-wise and we're reaping the benefits of me being a stay-at-home mum and a childminder.
Tammy from Runcorn, mum to Harry, five, and Madison, two

Looking for a new job

If you haven't been in work since you gave birth, or if you're returning to work after a career break, a start at school for your child might be just the catalyst that prompts you to go back. Unfortunately, many mums who are looking to return to work after a long break find their bridges are somewhat burned: their old position is long ago filled; few employers are offering the part-time hours they want; and former skills are in dire need of updating. Chances are, you're also going to be in need of a serious confidence boost, too.

Part-time work and job-shares can be hard to come by, so it's worth starting the search early. In particular, paid positions within schools, such as classroom or welfare assistants, secretaries, bursars, or lunchtime supervisors, are popular and almost always get loads of candidates when advertised. Still, it's worth considering. Don't hang around waiting for opportunities to arise, though – ask in the school office and make sure it's known that you'd be interested, should something crop up.

There are lots of useful online sources for job hunters, including specific information for mums who are heading back to the workplace. Some are included in the appendix at the back of the book.

Looking the part

Use a return to work, or job seeking, as a good excuse for an image update, if you need one. (If you're entering the school gate zone, you may want to give the yummy-mummy crew a small run for their money in any case.) Treat yourself to a new outfit or two, and maybe something a bit more daring than you've been used to – some killer heels, perhaps, or a cheeky hemline. If you're feeling a bit clueless because it's been a while, why not make use of a free personal shopping service, available in many department stores: there's no obligation to buy and you often get to enjoy a cup of tea while someone else does the hard work.

Sometimes a new haircut can do wonders for your confidence, so if you think you could do with a restyle or perhaps a colour update and the cost isn't prohibitive – go for it. If you are short of cash, perhaps you could ask for a makeover as part of a Christmas, birthday or Mother's Day present? At the very least, head for that department store again for a make-up demonstration, and maybe some free samples.

Polishing up your CV (and your brain)

You'll need to make sure your curriculum vitae is shipshape if you're in the job market. There are companies that will draw one up for you for a fee, but if you need a cheaper option, there's lots of advice and templates online. If you've got a friend who's good at these things, ask her to help, and make sure you get several sharp-eyed volunteers to read it for you.

Don't forget to include all your newly acquired 'mum skills' on your CV, as many are just what bosses are looking for in the workplace: OK, maybe they won't want to hear about your nappy-changing abilities, but great organisational skills, the ability to multi-task, fast reactions, problem-solving, thinking on your feet, managing a budget and working under pressure are likely to stand you in good stead.

Get your brain in gear and mug up if necessary: check out relevant publications or websites; find out about any new advances, big industry changes, relevant statistics or whatever will give you some background knowledge about your industry or sector. Find out what the latest computer programmes are and try to give them a whirl if you can. And if you're hoping to head back to the same job or even the same company, make contact with some old colleagues and pick their brains.

If you have training or were a bit of a high-flier before, maybe you can only find work that, frankly, you're overqualified for. You wouldn't be the first mum to take on a job that's a step down for the sake of your children, so try not to feel negatively about it. See it as a temporary measure that will allow you to spend a bit more time with your kids while they're little. There'll be time enough to return to something else a bit later on – but do make sure you get whatever fulfilment you need out of work hours, perhaps with a hobby you love.

Back to school for you, too

There are thousands of full- and part-time courses available these days (with financial help that you might well be eligible for on offer in some cases) to help you find your feet and boost your chances in the world of work-after-kids. So now could be the time to investigate adult education or re-training opportunities. In particular, you might want to find out some more about a government scheme called the Six Month Offer, which is a free retraining programme that promises to help you get the skills you want and that local employers are looking for, and to help you to work out an individual training plan.

Your local library is a good place to start if you're seeking information about what's available in your area, and there's loads of advice on the Direct Gov website.

Dr Bob says: Psychologically speaking, lack or loss of confidence is often a key factor in determining what we do with our lives and successfully accomplishing our aims. Countless studies have found that those who approach tasks with a high degree of confidence in their own success are much more likely to succeed than those with similar or even higher levels of ability or skill but less confidence.

Staying at home

Maybe you've no plans at all to work while your child is at school – maybe you're going to stay at home. This could be the case if you've got younger children to care for, or if you just want to make sure it's you that takes and collect from school and is around in the event of your child being poorly, or if your attendance is required at daytime events (of which there can be a surprising number). In fact, some mums actually *stop* work in order to be at home when their little one starts school, having gone back when they were babies, because they feel it's a time when they are particularly needed.

If you take this route, you may find the sudden change of lifestyle takes a bit of getting used to. If you worked and you've always thrived in company, or if you spent days with your little one that included a regular stream of coffee mornings and play dates, the house is going to feel pretty empty for a while. Even with the cleaning, shopping and household admin sorted, you might find yourself at a bit of a loose end.

Enjoy any free time you get: after all, it's the least you deserve if you've worked hard as a full-time mum, or if you've made sacrifices in order to be around for your child. Fill it with distracting pursuits like exercise, hobbies or meeting friends for lunch or coffee. Chances are that many of the mums you know will be working now, but there should be a new generation with younger kids that you can infiltrate. As ever, you can go online and check out the forums at Netmums if you're looking for buddies and aren't sure where to start.

Voluntary work, if you can spare the time, could also fill a few hours. In particular, you might want to ask about opportunities to be a parent helper at school: it's a great way to get involved. There's more about it on page 158.

What the netmums say

Staying at home

My son started school in September 2007 at our local infant school, when my daughter was only a few months old. My partner and I had actually put off having our second baby until our son would be starting school so that I would be on maternity leave when he did. I really wanted to be there to drop him off and collect him, maintain contact with the teachers and just generally be there to support him. I was hoping to go back to work part-time, but I wanted to continue with the school run, so I won't be returning until my daughter is settled in Reception. It means a lot to be able to do this and we are very lucky to be in a situation to be able to do so. I don't like the idea of having to drop my children at a breakfast club at 8am and collect them from an after-school club at 6pm – it's too much for them in my opinion – but everyone's circumstances are different and it's good that we have these options as parents.
Lisa from Cheltenham, mum to Alexander, seven, and Zoe, three

When my little boy started school I was working as a senior accountant and, because I considered starting school was such a milestone for my son, I took the decision to quit my job and I've never looked back. I just love it when I drop him off at school and tell him how much I love him and how proud I am of him. I adore it when I pick him up and we talk about his day and then go off to all sorts of after-school activities. Meanwhile I'm trying to set up an accounting and taxation business so I can work from home.
Maria from Ealing, mum to Marcus, four, and James, three

The first few weeks were a bit like I was waiting for the phone to ring! I think my son adapted to school better than I did. After I learnt to relax a bit, I would use my time to do things I enjoyed, like surfing the internet, reading, enjoying long baths in peace. I am also a parent helper on school trips whenever I can be and, of course, I do the odd bit of housework. Now I have another son, who is too young for nursery, so I spend my days playing with him. I'm qualified to be a childminder but the thought of Ofsted inspecting my home just makes me feel it's harder than it looks. Plus with two children of my own, I have my hands full.
Kate from Shrewsbury, mum to Jack, six, and Charlie, 18 months

I was at a bit of a loss at first when Martha started school – I was so used to having her around me all day long. I did find myself talking to myself in the supermarket a lot, and if another person's child said, 'Mummy', I'd automatically say, 'Yes, darling?', which was a bit embarrassing! I had the idea of drawing up a rota of things to do each day to fill the time and now I don't know how I managed to look after Martha full-time as I'm so busy!
Rachael from Twickenham, mum to Martha, five

I have my two-year-old daughter at home with me still, so it's nice to have her to myself as I've never had that – she's always had her brother around. I do get to do more cleaning as she likes to help and is easily amused, and I like to think I have a good balance.
Becky from Leeds, mum to Harry, four, and Bethany, two

Dr Bob says: For a stay-at-home parent, a child starting school is a much more important psychological issue than is sometimes recognised; it's the beginning of the 'empty nest' syndrome. Once the parent is satisfied that the child is settled at school (which may take days, weeks or even a few months) and provided that there are no other children awaiting their turn, then it is important to begin considering the next phase in his or her life.

5 Starting school

Welcome to the wonderful world of education

So the big day when your little one enters Reception is finally here. It's a major rite of passage and a real red-letter day for any family – one of those memories you're sure to look back on, possibly even something your little one will remember in adulthood – so you need to make it as positive an event as possible. There are still a few things you can do in the days leading up to the start that will help.

Getting to know teacher

Some Reception teachers will make a home visit, either just before your child starts school or during the first weeks of term (they can often be fitted in during normal school days because of the common practice of part-time starts). They're a great way for your child to make her teacher's acquaintance on an individual basis and in the secure and familiar setting of her own home ground.

Don't expect too much from your little one during this visit: even if she's not usually shy, she may well be on this occasion. If she makes herself scarce, refuses to speak or clings on to you like a limpet, bear in mind that this is usual – and the teacher won't make any assumptions or judgements based on it. Use the visit to pass on any information about your child that you think will be useful for them to know.

Meeting other parents and children beforehand

Some schools arrange a coffee morning or play session just before the first day (or perhaps just afterwards, if a part-time start allows for it) where fellow parents and children can meet and exchange contact information. As well as giving your child a chance to meet potential classmates ahead of the school start, it's also a great opportunity for you to start building your own support network. If your school doesn't offer this meeting opportunity, why not suggest it yourself – or just set one up informally.

Easing them in gently

Starting policies vary hugely among schools but, typically, there are staggered starts to allow an 'easing-in' period for Reception children, rather than a sudden leap into the full-time day. It may be that your child is invited to start some days or even weeks after the rest of the school, while many schools admit the Reception class on a part-time basis, having them in just for mornings or afternoons for a while. Sometimes the older half of the class (those with a birthday earlier in the school year) will start before the younger half, or the class is temporarily split into two, with half coming in the morning and half in the afternoon, giving teachers a good chance to get everyone settled.

Sometimes easing-in periods can be minimal: perhaps just a day or two of part-time, before going straight into full-time days. When this happens, some parents worry that it's too abrupt. On the other hand, others grumble when it's drawn out because it can be inconvenient and mean extra childcare is required. Either way, you'll have to assume that the school is doing whatever is thought to be the best option, and go with it.

If your little one has been attending a nursery class attached to the school during the previous year, easing in is going to be a simpler process: she'll be used to breezing her way through those gates of a morning and, unless the nursery's in a separate unit, she'll know her way around. Staff, even if they haven't been taught by them, will be familiar, as will the children in the classes above. Of course, she may have been at nursery on a part-time basis and so will still need to get to grips with full days – however, it's very likely she will also be offered a part-time start.

What the netmums say

All about staggered starts

After surviving the first four weeks of part-time schooling (a bone of contention with many working parents!) we have now settled into a routine that works well.

Ruth from Lancaster, mum to Jamie, four

The first term was mornings only and I couldn't find a suitable childminder, so Grace went to nursery in the afternoons with a combination of friends and my husband (on a long lunch break) picking her up from school and taking her there.

Sarah from Witham, mum to Grace, five, and Tom, two

My daughter's school seems to take the easing-in concept to extremes. All the Reception children are part-time for the

whole of the first term, with the younger ones in class in the mornings, and the older ones in during the afternoon. Then the older half of the class goes full-time in January, and the younger half after Easter. Personally I think it's good to give them loads of time and, as I work from home, it wasn't such a problem having her around in the mornings – I know it made life difficult for some people, though.
Julia from Milton Keynes, mum to Nina, seven, and Ellie, four

Emma says: Many children start school on a part-time basis for a number of weeks so you may need to make alternative childcare arrangements during this period if you work. It could mean continuing a private nursery place, looking for a childminder, taking time off work or asking family and friends for support. Speak to your chosen school as early as possible to discover what type of system they use. This will then give you time to make arrangements.

A few days before

Don't go on and on about her first day at school, but do give her a couple of gentle reminders that it's coming up soon. Perhaps she'll want to try her uniform on again (some children seem to enjoy doing this repeatedly in the run-up to school starting!), or maybe you can chat about what she might find in the classroom when she gets there.

Get all the practical preparations sorted a few days in advance – you don't want to leave it until the day before, or worse, the morning itself and then be running around like a headless chicken when you need to be calm and organised. Make sure her uniform is labelled, pressed and hung up or folded, and get her bag ready, if she needs one. Involve your little one as much as possible – let her fold some of her clothes and give her shoes a buffing with a soft cloth.

You might want to shop for a small present to give her on her first morning: if there's a possibility she'll want to take it in, make it small and practical – perhaps a key-ring with a soft toy attached that she can clip to the zip of her bag. Do resist the temptation to pack her off with her favourite cuddly: most schools have a policy on children bringing toys in to school as they can be a distraction and are likely to get lost or taken home by another child (although some teachers are lenient on this, usually on the proviso it's put away in a box or cupboard on arrival).

If you feel there'll be strength in numbers, liaise with parents of any friends she has joining at the same time. You could perhaps arrange to travel to school together on the first day, or to meet up outside so they can go in at the same time.

The day before

Make the day and evening before the first day as calm as you possibly can. Spend the day doing something interesting (but not exhausting) to keep worries at bay. Then get her clothes and bag laid out, and aim for a bath and an early night, with some time devoted to a bedtime story and a chat. Ask if she's looking forward to it. Say you are and that you can't wait to see her looking grown-up in her school uniform.

On the day

You may have a few nerves when you wake up, but you won't be the only parent to feel that way. Focus on the practical things you need to do and be your usual cheery self without going over the top with enthusiasm: most kids can tell a fake a mile off!

Get up a bit earlier than you need to and spend a little time waking your child gently. Don't worry if she doesn't fancy much for breakfast: she might have a few butterflies in her tummy. If she can't eat, a glass of milk or a cup of hot chocolate will keep her going. Once she's dressed and ready, take a few photos of her in her uniform, if she's not too reluctant! Otherwise, take the camera in and you can snap her on her way into school. Give her hugs and reassurance if she seems at all upset, but don't smother her or make her feel like leaving you is going to be a really big deal. If you're anxious, try not to show it: be perky and positive. Tell her you remember your first day at school and that even though you were a bit nervous at first it was fine within a very short time of arriving.

Make mornings bearable

Start as you mean to go on in the mornings, with everything organised as far as possible the night before, so you can have a calm approach to getting ready. You're about to discover that life can get pretty hectic prior to leaving the house. So set up a star chart or similar reward scheme to encourage her to get dressed and ready on time, and stick a list to the fridge door to remind you of what's happening on what day, and what needs taking to school and when. It'll be less of an issue at the start, but as time goes on (and with subsequent children also at school) you'll find there are more and more things to pack and to remember – PE kits, permission forms, special events, reading books, homework sheets and much more! You need a good system to help you keep it all in check.

At the school

Come the first day, you might be invited to take your little one into the class and perhaps to hang around for a little while. But that will usually only be the first day – after that most teachers would prefer you to deliver your child to the school door and shoot off fairly swiftly, because it's actually easier for them to get on with settling children, and dealing with any upset ones, if parents are not around. (And some will want you to do that from day one, in any case. Do this if they request it, however much you're tempted to linger.)

You'll no doubt be informed what the procedure is for getting children into school. There may be different entrances, or different times for different year groups to make their entrance.

Parting for the first time might be difficult, for one or both of you. It's a rare parent who doesn't feel a little emotional on the approach to school – try not to cry if you can possibly help it, at least until she's safely inside. You'll probably see other equally fragile-looking parents and you can all support each other later on.

Try to be businesslike while remaining cheerful and encouraging. Don't rush your child away from you, but don't cling to her either. If she looks very insecure, distract her by talking about the playground equipment or pointing out other children's bags or lunchboxes. And if she's the one who's feeling more relaxed than you are, try not to look to her for reassurance: it can be all too easy to transfer negative feelings by saying, 'Won't you miss Mummy, then?' or 'I thought you weren't looking forward to this!'

When it comes to saying goodbye, try not to make it protracted: give one quick kiss or hug, tell her you'll see her later (which is more reassuring than 'goodbye') and don't look back as you make your exit. In most cases, she'll be fine within a few minutes.

Don't leave me!

Some kids are absolutely fine about being left at school on the first day – in fact, some don't even look back. But for many it's a difficult experience and for some, it is downright traumatic.

Distressing as it can be to have to leave a sobbing or terrified child, you will have to be strong about peeling them off your leg and walking away: remind yourself that it's a short-term reaction and that your little one is soon going to be having a wonderful time. You'll almost certainly be leaving her in good hands. As a rule Reception teachers and their assistants are incredibly sympathetic, sensitive professionals and – unless they are new to the job themselves – they're going to know all about dealing with anxious children who don't want their mummies to leave them. Most will take a firm but kind approach to an unhappy child: they are generally willing to get involved if a child needs physically prising apart from you, but you can be certain that no one is going to be unkind to your little one at a time when she's so distressed.

If you don't have work to go to, do something other than going home alone: go for a coffee with some of the other mums; take yourself off shopping; go for a swim or a run – anything to keep yourself occupied.

Chances are she'll come out of school full of all the news about her day and her new friends – but if she is subdued or says she doesn't want to go back again, reassure her that it's quite normal for her to feel that way, and that she'll feel happy at school very soon.

Emma says: I personally wouldn't find it helpful for a parent to hang around on the first day, as it may make it harder for a child to settle if they're hanging on to their mummy. For your own sake, try to find out if your school offers a 'first day coffee morning'. This can be a great way to meet other parents and ease your nerves. You could even offer to help run one if the school seems amenable to the idea.

Dr Bob says: Many cases of separation anxiety emanate from the mother rather than from the child. Young children pick up non-verbal as well as verbal cues remarkably quickly. If a mother is anxious about her child's welfare or reluctant to 'let go', this may be passed on to her child and manifest itself as 'school phobia'.

What the netmums say

The very first day

Natasha started school in January and, as luck would have it, there was the added excitement and distraction of thick snow having settled overnight. Her dad made a tiny snowman in our porch before we set off, so she was all giggles and wonderment. I have a lovely photo of her standing next to the snowman in her oversized uniform, clutching her Winnie-the-Pooh lunchbox and grinning from ear to ear. When we got to the school she was a bit tearful, but as soon as she spotted her friend from nursery she was OK again and settled in very happily over the next few days. She's never looked back.
Helen from Harrow, mum to Natasha, five

I arranged for my friend, who actually lives a few miles away, to meet us at our house with her daughter, who was in Year 2, so that my son had someone already at the school to go in with. He really seemed to appreciate it and my friend's daughter felt very grown-up chaperoning Ryan in on his first day. It's something we've repeated if there's a difficult day ahead – like when he's going back after half term and feeling a bit anxious again.
Maura from Newport, mum to Ryan, five

On the first day of school I gave my little boy a kiss on the palm of his hand and told him if he missed me at all during the day he could kiss his own palm and it would be like getting a kiss from me. He probably never needed to do it, but it made me feel a bit better waving him off!
Catriona from Glengormley, mum to Fintan, five, and Connor, two

Harry has been finding it hard because one of his best friends from pre-school isn't joining the infants until after Easter, but I've told him it's something to look forward to, and he's actually fine once he gets there. The times he gets upset about missing her are when he's really tired.
Becky from Leeds, mum to Harry, four, and Bethany, two

My daughter was quite blasé about starting. But there was one little girl who was really traumatised. She screamed for her mum every day, for at least the first fortnight. I heard that the teaching assistant got kicked quite hard by her at one point, but was totally unfazed. All part of life in Reception, I guess.
Donna from Bingley, mum to Jade, seven, and Billie, three

Inside the Reception class

You may find that your child's classroom looks very different to the one you remember from starting school yourself. With the emphasis of the Early Years Foundation Stage on learning through play, it's likely to look more like a nursery set-up than a conventional schoolroom, with little in the way of tables and chairs, and a range of clearly defined areas: typically there will be some kind of role play corner with props;

a creative corner; a clear space for 'carpet-time'; a 'quiet' or reading zone; and some kind of outdoor play area. You'll almost certainly notice one or more computers in the room, and in most schools now, where you might once have seen a blackboard, there'll be an interactive white board – a large display screen that connects to a computer and projector. You're also likely to see a large selection of toys, dressing-up clothes, lots of art supplies, musical instruments and audio equipment, and resources for sand and water play. There should also be loads of wonderful work displayed on the walls and perhaps hanging from the ceiling.

There's more about the specifics of the Early Years Foundation Stage curriculum on page 134.

Who's who at school?

The most important person in school for your child is the Reception class teacher. Hopefully you'll have met her at least once and you feel confident your little one is in good hands. If you don't feel you know them well, or you're not sure you like them, try to bear in mind that – as a rule – Reception year teachers are kind, sympathetic people who will know exactly what your little one is going through and will have lots of strategies for making her transition from pre-schooler to pupil as enjoyable and pain-free as possible. She may or may not have a role as the school's Early Years Foundation Stage Co-ordinator, giving her overall responsibility for all children and staff in the Early Years Foundation Stage. Your child may also be allocated a 'key person', who has special responsibilities for working with them and building a relationship with you. Most likely it will be the teacher herself, or it could be a member of the support staff.

Sometimes teaching positions are shared by two part-time teachers, so your child may have different teachers on different days. It can take a while to work out who's in charge on which days – some parents never quite get to grips with this detail! – and you may worry that this arrangement will lack continuity and be to your child's disadvantage. But as long as both teachers are organised and communicate well (which they usually will be if they want their jobshare to work), there's no reason to feel negatively about it.

Your child may also have to get to know a regular stand-in teacher. All teachers can use ten per cent of their teaching time out of the classroom concentrating on planning, preparation and assessment (PPA). This period might be covered by a regular supply teacher, a teacher from another class, a part-time teacher whose job is to cover all PPA sessions, or the teaching assistant (TA).

Increasingly these days, with teachers pushed for time and tied up in paperwork, the TA plays a vital role, often far beyond just helping with reading and mopping up mess. Also known sometimes as classroom assistants or learning support assistants, TAs aren't required to have formal qualifications but many now do. They may be in the classroom on a full-time basis but aren't ever required to lead a lesson, although they may well be in charge of the class for short periods if the teacher isn't around. You should certainly get an introduction to the Reception class TA in the early days – if you haven't already – so make sure you know who she is and be sure to put yourself on good terms with her. It may well be that if you've got a query or concern, she is quite able to help you with it, and may just have a little more time to do so. And she's very likely to be the person who gives your little one reassurance or help if she's upset, hurt, or has had an 'accident'.

Other important members of staff include the head teacher, school secretary, bursar, caretaker, and lunchtime or playground supervisors. The rest of the school's teachers are also likely to have prominent roles around the school, for instance holding assemblies or doing playground supervision. And if your child has any special needs, she (and you) will also get to know the school's Special Educational Needs Co-ordinator, who could be any one of the teachers there (there's more on special educational needs on page 35). There's very likely, too, to be a number of volunteer helpers (usually parents), who might be around helping her with reading or artwork, changing books, or supervising her play activities.

What will my child be doing all day?

You might be surprised – and pleased – by the relaxed nature of the day your child spends in the classroom during her first year at school. As a rule there's little in the way of structured teaching in Reception, with children often encouraged to be 'free range', moving around the room at will to enjoy all the different areas of play, and coming together at times for guided whole-group activities. At some point, they'll be encouraged to shift their play outside, too.

Reception teachers have to use the Early Years Foundation Stage (EYFS), which is part of the National Curriculum, to guide them in all the activities they set – if your little one went to a registered pre-school setting, she'll already have spent her days under its guidance. (For more on the EYFS see page 4.)

In many cases, activities will tick the box of more than one of these areas at a time, and teachers often look for ways that they can make learning 'cross-curricular'. For example, a group of children building with blocks may be co-operating in who carries what, negotiating the best place to put them, comparing their weights and dimensions, and pretending to be Bob the Builder while they're at it. So they're developing their language, mathematical, physical and personal and social skills through one activity.

If you want to know more about the specifics of your child's day and what her learning and play will involve, her teacher should be glad to talk to you about it. There's more on the subject of communicating with teachers in the following chapter.

Learning goals

There are early learning goals that teachers must aim to help your child achieve by the end of the Early Years Foundation Stage (in other words, at the end of Reception year), for which children are assessed throughout the year, very informally and through observation by staff. They'll use their assessments to help them complete an Early Years Foundation Stage Profile for each child, which outlines their progress in all these areas, mainly with the purpose of providing information about a child for their Year 1 teacher, when the time comes for them to move up from Reception. (Inevitably, this system comes in for a fair bit of criticism from those who feel teachers would be better off spending all their time interacting with children of this age, rather than wasting some of it on assessments and form-filling.) You'll be given a copy of this profile yourself at the end of the year. The goals include a huge range of expected achievements, for example: being able to sing a simple song from memory; recognising numerals from one to nine; taking turns and sharing fairly; and being able to read a range of familiar and common words.

Of course, they don't just get to these goals through their learning at school, they get to them with help from you, too. There's more about what you can do at home to support and boost your child's learning, in Reception and beyond, in the following chapter.

Food for thought

Please don't expect too much of me
I'm learning more than you can see.
Being simply here to enjoy and play
Means more to me than I can say
Please don't fret at the end of the day
If I have nothing to display.

I really gain so much from play
Social skills and come what may
So when I come home empty handed
From such a very busy play
Please don't say
Haven't you done anything today?

Emma says: Quite a few schools actually put their curriculum planning on the school website so you can view what the children will be getting up to throughout the year. Some schools even have a curriculum evening part way through the autumn term to explain how the curriculum works, the methods they will be using and where you can find more information. It's also worth checking out the curriculum websites so that you familiarise yourself with some of the terminology. Many classes will also have a termly newsletter so that you can look at what they will be learning about over the coming weeks. But overall, the best way to find out more about what's happening in the classroom is to have a chat with the teacher. She or he should certainly be happy to talk you through the way in which the curriculum works, although they may prefer to do this in a parent meeting. Another good way to find out about what your child is learning is to volunteer, if you have the time, so that you are able to spend some time in the classroom.

Settling in

With any luck, your child will quickly settle happily into school life and without heartache. But some new joiners do find it hard to settle. If your child doesn't know any of the other children, she may find it harder to make new friends, especially if lots of the children already know one another; she may find she doesn't particularly gel with her new teacher; she might feel intimated by being around so many people at once – especially if she hasn't experienced a playgroup or nursery setting beforehand; the school building will probably feel very large and imposing to her, however tiny it felt to you when you visited; or she might be reluctant to speak up if she needs something – and, in the case of the loo, this may result in an embarrassing accident.

Settling problems can also sneak up further on in the term, when a child who settles well initially shows signs of anxiety or reluctance a little later. Usually this is because reality has hit home: they're in school full-time and they're there to stay!

Regressing and playing up

Just as your child may have shown signs of regression in the run-up to starting school, these first early days and weeks are another time during which you might notice a few backslides. For instance, you may get a return (where they have previously stopped) to issues such as bedwetting, thumb-sucking, tantrums, mild sleep disturbances, soiling and clinginess, or other babyish demands for your time and attention. Your best strategy is to be sympathetic but practical – don't overdo the cosseting and 'poor baby' comments. On the other hand, don't show disapproval or try to force her into getting over it: either strategy is likely to backfire. Deal with these problems in a matter-of-fact way and she should soon move through it.

Let these things take their course and pledge just to see how things are in a few weeks' time: chances are she'll have moved on. If you're really concerned, chat to her teacher to see if there are any particular problems at school, or if there's anything they can suggest to help. Primary school teachers are almost always excellent child psychologists on the side, and will very often have some useful ideas.

They'll certainly be in touch with you if they notice any problems at school and feel there's something that you need to tackle.

Carrying the can at home

You may well notice a decline in behaviour at home once your little one starts school. It's incredibly common and is probably because they are having to be so good for their teacher all the time that they need an outlet for all the frustrations and difficult feelings they are having to keep a lid on – not to mention the fact that they're probably exhausted. (The positive flipside is that you could find yourself relieved to hear that the child you thought was prone to cheekiness, tantrums, stubbornness or lack of enthusiasm is, in fact, an all-round delight as far as their teacher is concerned!)

Try to give her some slack for bad behaviour at home in the period after starting school, without letting your usual rules and boundaries slide completely. Meanwhile, allow her loads of rest and relaxation time after school and at the weekends, and make sure she's getting early nights and plenty of sleep.

There's more about dealing with overtiredness on page 142.

What the netmums say

Settling-in issues

My daughter had only turned four in June, but she absolutely loved starting school. On the second day, as I was about to walk her to her classroom, she turned to me and said, 'I can do it myself, Mummy.' I remember thinking to myself, 'I've taken two weeks off work to make sure you settle in OK and you have already!'

Jacqui from Gravesend, mum to Lois, six

For the first two weeks, Megan was just doing afternoons. She was clingy at the gate, as were some of the others, but she seemed to be the only one after those weeks who was still being this way. Thankfully she settled down eventually. She has always been a thumbsucker – mainly when she's tired – so we weren't surprised when she carried on sucking her thumb, but we did have quite a few occurrences of bedwetting during the first month. Again, thankfully this has settled down now.
Carrie'ann from Wakefield, mum to Megan, four

When my daughter started Reception last September, aged five, I found it very hard to get any information from her as to how she was getting on: 'Can't remember, don't know' was the usual sort of reply. We started a little ritual at teatime where each person says their favourite and least favourite thing that has happened during the day. My little three-and-a-half-year-old also joins in and I have found out so much from both of them about their school/nursery day. It just starts off the conversation and they seem to open up more.
Colleen from Colchester, mum to Samantha, five, and Thomas, three

As I'm a working mum, my daughter had been attending nursery from the age of two and a half, so she was all ready for the separation – or so I thought! It actually took several weeks for her to settle and we had lots of tears on both sides. We ended up agreeing with the teacher that Scarlett could take a comfort toy in, and the teacher emailed me a picture of her after I'd left to show she was settling OK.
Clare from Lincoln, mum to Scarlett, five

When my daughter started full-time school in September, I thought I would be fine with her going all day as she had been to nursery at the school for the last half of the previous school year. But when it came to it, I still felt as though she was entering a new world where I could no longer control or keep her safe. She would be doing new things I wasn't involved in, meeting new people who I couldn't vet, choosing things for herself . . . As much as I tried to tell myself she was ready for it emotionally and mentally, she is still and will always remain my little girl! Nearly six months on I am very happy to report I have got over myself. I've realised she needs me just as much but in a different way. I'm helping her forge new friendships by stepping back and allowing her to choose her friends. I'm helping her develop by encouraging learning (I'm very proud of her reading) and extending the learning at home that she has started at school. So I realise my job is not redundant – it's merely moved on to the next journey we're taking together.
Vikki from Bradford, mum to Joseie, five

Both my girls started so well, but then when the novelty wore off the worries crept in as well as the realisation that this was every day except weekends and there was no going back. I dealt with this with lots of reassurance, lots of saying, 'You have to go and it will get better', and lots of relaxation at weekends. I'd advise any parent to be prepared for a wobble a couple of weeks in when they suddenly realise that school is for the foreseeable future and not just an exciting first few days.
Nicola from Edinburgh, mum to Hannah, eight, and Feena, six

After nursery, where I had lots of feedback, I realised I didn't even know what time my daughter was eating lunch, let

alone what she was doing all day. Due to the child to teacher ratio, the feedback is a lot less, which I wasn't prepared for. Now that we are in the second term it's getting easier and we are coming up to a second parents' evening. So overall it has been a learning curve for us both and as long as you try to make the challenges for them as easy as possible by remembering everything and making sure they have what they need, it does get easier.
Melani from Chester, mum to Kendall, five

Emma says: Often a short chat with the teacher can help to reassure you or deal with any concerns that you may have. Teachers are very aware that the first few months at school can be a little confusing and tiring for some children, so they will want to work with you to ensure that your child settles well and feels comfortable.

Dr Bob says: Children and families function best within a generally understood and accepted set of routines. A child starting school will almost certainly disrupt established routines in some way. Parents need to recognise this and decide how to readjust their routines accordingly. Another factor to take into account is the issue of time. At home a child is likely to have considerable freedom to decide what to do, when to eat and when to request (or even demand!) individual attention. The regime of school life is very different and is structured around set time periods, required patterns of behaviour and having to share adult attention with 20 or more others.

After school

Your little one is likely to be totally exhausted after school, and particularly at the end of the week. Tiredness can manifest itself in different ways: some children just want cuddles and some quiet time when they get home; others might be unusually grumpy or impatient; some will happily go to bed earlier than usual; others get over-tired which, conversely, can make them hyperactive.

If she does any activities outside of school, like swimming or ballet, it might be wise to drop them temporarily while she adjusts to the demands of her new routine. It certainly wouldn't be a good idea to take up any new ones. Similarly, do limit play dates. Ideally she should have no more than a couple of days when she's doing something after school: let her do absolutely nothing, except perhaps soak up a bit of television, on as many afternoons as possible. If you're lucky enough to be at home with her in those after-school hours, and you've got the luxury of a bit of time to spare, try to cuddle up and watch it with her for a bit. It's a great excuse for a breather for you and a lovely bit of comfort for her.

You may find she's famished after school, even after a snack, and this, combined with an early bedtime looming, means you may have to look at a fairly early teatime in the week. This is a bit of a nuisance if you like to eat together as a family and 5.30–6pm is either too early or just not practical for you. If you do have to eat later, try and sit down with her while she and any siblings eat, and talk and snack while she has hers. Now's a good time to chat about the day – but don't push her for details if she's not volunteering them, and talk about other things apart from school, too.

As for homework, well, hopefully there'll be very little to tackle during her Reception year, beyond a little regular reading practice and the odd simple, practical task. In any case, it's always a good idea to get this done earlier rather than later when she's tired (and you are, too). And getting it done early is a good habit to get into because in later school years there'll be significant amounts to plough through and, as you no doubt remember from your own school days, it's never a good idea to leave homework until the last minute. There's more about homework on page 170.

A daily bath might be part of the routine in your house – though as time goes on, and homework and extra-curricular activities start to enter the frame, you may well find this is one of things that goes by the wayside. Encourage her to fold whatever uniform is still clean and put it out for the morning, and get her to help you get bags, shoes and whatever else will be needed lined up.

Bedtimes are all-important in helping her adapt to her new schedule: try to stick to one during this period. In fact, keep it up indefinitely and it will pay dividends for you both. If you need to, bring bedtime forward and make time for a longer period of settling down. A bath, perhaps with a few drops of lavender oil in it, a warm milky drink, or a story CD might help. Try to make sure she's in bed with the lights out by 7.30pm – busy schoolchildren need to get a full night's sleep.

There's a bit more about this on page 86 and lots more good ideas for bedtime in the sleep pages at Netmums.

What the Netmums say

Coping with tiredness

Oddly enough, I've found Jamie to be more tired on a Monday than on a Friday. We've dealt with this by just having 'quiet time' after school on these days. He can get a little tetchy when he's tired, so I've picked up on these cues.

Ruth from Lancaster, mum to Jamie, four

> Lena was really grumpy for the first three or four weeks and it took me a while to realise that she was exhausted. After a couple of weeks, though, I stopped her going to after-school clubs temporarily, brought her whole evening routine forward by half an hour and let her enjoy a bit more time in bed in the mornings by making a simpler breakfast.
> *Angela from Worthing, mum to Lena, five*

Making friends

Hopefully your little one had a few friends already when she started school and, even if she didn't, she should form a few tentative bonds in the early days and weeks. Small children are sociable creatures, as a rule, and even if the thought of plunging into a 30-strong group of new faces makes you feel a bit queasy, chances are she'll take it in her stride. She may well latch on to one or two particular pals, but don't worry if she seems a bit obsessed with so-and-so in the early days, she'll almost certainly move on and make new friends with time.

If she's very shy or just has a reserved personality, your child might struggle to form friendships. If you're worried, have a chat to her teacher. She'll have strategies to help and, in fact, she's more than likely putting them in place, anyway. Meanwhile, try not to worry and give her lots of extra love at home.

> ***Emma says:*** If your child is shy, don't be afraid to ask the class teacher whom they have noticed them playing with and start by talking to your child about these children. It may be that they would like to invite one of them to play but haven't found the confidence to mention it.

Making friends (for you)

If you're a school newbie yourself, you may be suffering from shyness, or feeling left out and convinced that everyone else is already in an impenetrable clique. You won't be alone, so perhaps you could seek out a mum who also seems a little lonely and strike up conversation?

Some mums do find it really hard integrating: if this is you, remind yourself that by befriending a few other mums, you might make friends for your child, too. You'll also be in a good position to offer, and ask for, favours if you need to. If you're finding it hard to strike up conversations with another mum, an easy starting point is to chat or ask questions about their child. And acting as if you're confident can really give you the feeling that you are: so pull those shoulders back, put on a cheery expression and walk purposefully towards whoever you want to approach.

One thing's for sure, there are plenty of people around with whom you have a big thing in common: little ones who've just started school. Now that's a good talking point! There's more about school gate friendships and how to make them in Chapter 6.

6 Getting the best out of school life

Getting out what you put in

Once your little one has settled into school, you can shift your focus onto getting the very best out of his school life. That might include helping him with learning or other experiences, getting on well with staff, becoming involved or offering help yourself, and successfully interacting with other parents and their children.

These early days of education should be memorable for you – for all the right reasons – and hopefully you'll look back on your child's primary years with real affection. How much you get out of it, though, depends largely on how much you're prepared to put in: getting involved and showing an interest means his primary school days are more likely to be a positive experience, for both of you. And if you know you've done your best in that respect, then all those special moments – that first nativity, the summer fête, all his achievements, from the first gold star to his virtuoso performance at the recorder assembly – will be all the sweeter.

Playing by the rules

Every school has its own set of rules and they'll have been laid down for a reason: often they're there for health and safety reasons; or they may be simple matters of respect and discipline. Some rules are set in stone, others are really just guidelines that you are politely requested to abide by. Either way, you'd be wise to toe the line. Flouting school rules – even if some of them do seem arbitrary or petty – is likely to make you unpopular with staff, especially if you end up inspiring other parents to follow suit.

You'll find the rules of the school within the prospectus or on its website, and you're very likely to get frequent reminders via school newsletters. In some schools, pupils (and parents) are even required to sign an agreement to abide by the school's rules: this helps to reinforce how important they are to the successful running of the school and makes children feel that they have given some sort of commitment.

If you want to raise an issue over a school rule, you could email or chat to the head about it, or do so more formally by bringing it up at a PTA meeting, at a parent council, if your school has one, or in writing to the chairman of governors. You might want to garner some support from other parents if you really think a rule needs to be re-examined.

Golden guidelines: what teachers really need you to do for them

Make him attend (unless you've a good reason not to)

As a parent, you are legally responsible for making sure your child attends school. And attendance is a big deal at all schools: Ofsted reports assess absence levels and, by law, schools must do their best to keep them down. Illness, medical or dental appointments, religious celebrations and bereavement are considered acceptable reasons for missing school – anything else will require advance authorisation from the head (you may have to do this in writing or by filling in a special form). Follow the school's procedure for notifying illness: most will prefer you to let them know the same day by telephone, and you must send him back with a written note, or doctor's note if applicable, as schools are required by law to record these.

Keep him home if he's contagious

It's generally down to you to decide whether your child is too poorly to stay at home from school or not, but in the case of certain infectious diseases, for example scarlet fever, mumps, rubella, measles and chickenpox, you have a duty to notify the school and abide by whatever period of exclusion they recommend. In the case of diarrhoea and vomiting, you'll usually be asked to keep him home for 48 hours after his last episode.

Get him there on time

Every single day there'll be at least a handful of parents rushing their children through the school gates after the bell's gone – and, let's face it, who hasn't been there? But being significantly late without good reason, or very frequently late, is a real pain for teachers – it disrupts the class when a kid turns up halfway through the morning and they'll have to go over stuff they've already been through. It can also be embarrassing for your child. So set that alarm and pledge to get to school on time every day. Doing as much preparation as you can the night before is the best way to help you achieve this.

Don't take your holidays in term time

It's a subject that can cause a fair bit of grumbling at the school gates but, the fact is, teachers really need you not to take your child out of school for high days and holidays, for pretty obvious reasons – your child could miss out on important learning. Schools can use their discretion to grant up to ten days' authorised absence in a school year, so long as you apply in advance and there are 'special reasons' for the holiday. For a holiday of more than ten days, you'll be asked to show that it's because of 'exceptional circumstances'.

Abide by the uniform rules (and that means NO jewellery!)

Uniform is considered an important rule for most schools. Apart from anything else, it's going to make your child feel odd if he isn't dressed the same way as everyone else. A 'no jewellery' rule is usual in most schools for health and safety reasons (with the possible exception of a shatter-proof watch). Earrings, in particular, may need to be taken out or covered with plasters (if not generally, then certainly at PE times). Do take this into account if you're considering getting your child's ears pierced, as the original earrings have to be kept in for six weeks: get it done at the beginning of the summer holidays.

Leave their personal effects behind

Don't let him take in toys or anything else that matters, unless invited to or if you know there's a special box or cupboard it can go into when he gets there. Personal possessions are a nuisance because they can distract from learning and have a tendency to get lost or pinched.

Keep your nits to yourself

Outbreaks of head lice are par for the course at primary school and once one kid has them, they can quickly spread to others. It's down to you as a parent to regularly check your little one's hair (it's best done in the bath, with a fine-toothed nit comb and lots of conditioner) and tackle them if they do make an appearance, using a medicated lotion recommended by the chemist, or with a committed programme of combing them out. It's not usual, but some schools may ask a child with lice to stay away until they're gone.

Label *everything*!

Lost property is a major hassle for teachers. Make sure everything's labelled so that if it goes astray, it will either find its way back to your child, or you can easily claim it from the lost property box.

Read your newsletter

It's sent home to give you useful information, not for you to scribble your shopping list on the back. And it's worth searching through your child's bag for any letters which may have been sent home – young children are notorious for forgetting all about things like this!

Getting on well with teachers

Hang around a school or a teacher long enough and you're likely to hear the buzz-phrase 'parents as partners'. It's considered a crucial element of one of the Early Years Foundation Stage's four major themes – positive relationships – and it refers to the idea that, when it comes to early years education, it's a combination of teachers and parents working together that gives a child the best chance of doing well at school. Your child's teacher is likely to be very well tuned into this theory – hence, they'll consider your views and input important and, equally, will want to keep you well informed, through a variety of means, as to your child's progress, or indeed, any issues that need addressing.

What that means, more than anything, is that good communication between home and school is vital. Teaching staff will always be (or *should* always be) happy to hear your concerns and will appreciate any positive input you have to make. There are some things they won't appreciate, however: pushiness or downright interference in the way in which they teach and organise the children being one of them (after all, they're the experts). Bad timing is also a bugbear: the last thing teachers want is to be nabbed by a parent at the beginning of the school day, just when they are busy preparing the classroom for the day's lessons or getting the children into class and registration. So wait until after school if you want to talk to them and, better still, make a call or send an email or short note requesting a bit of their time, either direct or via the school secretary. Bear in mind that different schools are likely to have different approaches to this: some are happy for a fairly informal approach, with parents welcome to wander in off the cuff to have their say, while others will prefer you to go through a certain procedure.

There might also be other initiatives within the school, such as homework diaries or reading records via which you can also communicate with your child's teacher – these are there for your benefit and your child's, so do make the most of them. Do, do, DO read every spit and splutter contained in the school newsletter when you get one, and file it in a really obvious place (such as on the fridge door). School staff hate it when they're asked for information they've already outlined in great detail on a letter they've already sent home. And do make sure you and/or your partner attend every parents' evening that crops up. These are often held termly and give you a chance to talk with your child's teacher, see his work, find out about any targets that have been set for him and put any questions of your own.

Don't forget to be nice to your child's teacher, even if you don't have anything specific you need to discuss with them: a smile and wave first thing in the morning will go a long way. Aim to be on smiling terms with other teachers and support staff, too – after all, your little one may be under their care eventually – as well as the head, who'll usually be pretty visible and accessible in a primary school: make a point of saying hello if you pass.

Thank you, miss

It's very common practice in primary schools now for children to show their appreciation by bringing a card and/or a small gift for their teacher on the last day of term – certainly at the end of the school year, but very often for Christmas, too (and even at Easter). It's worth remembering that this is definitely not compulsory – if you could do without the expense, no one will think any worse of you. But if you are keen to show you care, bear in mind that – although teachers generally appreciate the gesture – the backlog of chocolates, candles and bubble bath may not necessarily be what they'd choose themselves. A great idea is to pool contributions with other parents and get a voucher instead. There's also a good chance they'll be glad of a bottle of wine – it's hard work teaching small kids, after all! (The school secretary will almost certainly be able to let you know if they are teetotal or not.)

The school office

The office is probably the school's hub and likely to be your first port of call for myriad enquiries or tasks, as well as the place your child may end up if he's hurt or unwell or has lost something. Most parent veterans of the primary school system will tell you it's worth being on good terms with the secretary and anyone else in the admin team. Chances are you'll be asking them for favours, such as passing on your child's packed lunch if it gets left at home, or forwarding a message or a forgotten form to a teacher. Some school secretaries are more approachable than others – and it has to be said that they are *sometimes* a little scary! But this will usually be because they are busy people, with a stressful role, so try, if at all possible, to bear that in mind. And try not to catch them at their busiest times of day (probably first and last thing in the day, and at lunchtime).

When something's wrong

Most teachers are enthusiastic professionals who care about their kids and are easy to get on with, too. Unfortunately – as in any walk of life – a few aren't. If you have a personality clash going on with your child's teacher, or even if you feel they are in some way failing to do their job properly, there's not a lot you can do about it: it's the luck of the draw. The odds are that it will be a one-off and your child's next teacher will be a good 'un. Meanwhile, grit your teeth and do the best you can to get on with them.

If you're significantly unhappy and you want to take action, do always go to the teacher first with your concerns rather than trying to go over their head to see someone with more seniority, as it's bound to cause bad feeling. If that doesn't resolve things, make an appointment to see the head about it. It's unlikely, but if the issue persists beyond that, you should ask to see, or look online for, a copy of the school's complaints procedure and go from there.

What the netmums say

Getting along with teacher

I don't feel I've built any relationships with the teachers. It's a very different experience from nursery, where you go in every night for a chat about the day, and I have found this quite difficult to adjust to. When you do make the effort to chat you don't always feel the teachers have the time. And I haven't been able to offer my services as I work full-time.
Clare from Lincoln, mum to Scarlett, five

We have found our child's teacher easy to talk to and approach about everyday things and any major issues that arise. Information is exchanged frequently via the telephone or in her home-school book, and I feel this is an advantage as questions and comments are shared easily and neither ourselves nor the teacher are in too much of a rush, so things can be discussed properly.
Nicola from Redcar, mum to Natasha, five

I'd never met the original Reception teacher as she was off with illness for a year. I met the other teachers at the meeting before they started school. When the original teacher came back just before Christmas, there was obvious tension. She'd never met me and didn't know my children like the other teachers did. We have clashed: she's very stern and can be quite short with the parents. One of my daughters shut down emotionally recently because this teacher had 'shouted' at her. I spoke to the

teacher but she has that air about her that makes you very nervous! Luckily it appears to be sorted now but I still don't really like her. I have to say I prefer the other teachers.
Abi from Chester, mum to Amy, five, and Jessica, two

My daughter's teacher is lovely – very approachable and a good listener who takes on board what parents have to say. She is quite young with young children of her own, and is strict but fair and very friendly. We have quite a few parents' consultation dates so we always receive a lot of info, and we get a lot of letters home, too.
Leanne from Wakefield, mum to Caris, five

I've tried to strike a balance between being interested in Natasha's progress and being a pushy parent – and it can be quite a fine line, I think. Natasha was struggling with number work at first, so instead of steaming in and criticising the teaching, I asked her teacher to give me some pointers as to how I could best help at home. I think the teacher appreciates this kind of co-operative approach, and I'm sure it works out better all round.
Helen from Harrow, mum to Natasha, five

Getting involved

There's not a state school in the country that doesn't need or appreciate voluntary help and support from its parents. You may have a lot of time to spare and you may have very little, but if you can make some kind of contribution beyond dropping off and picking up your child, there'll be benefits all round.

Joining the PTA

If you're really keen to get involved and you've got a bit of time to spare, you should definitely consider signing up for the PTA (Parent Teacher Association). The PTA is a body made up of parents and teachers, typically with a view to forging understanding between parents and school, raising funds, helping out at school trips, and organising events, in and out of school time. Regular meetings bring parents and teachers together in an informal atmosphere to exchange ideas about what will benefit the children and the school. Not all schools have a PTA, but they're a great bonus: if your's doesn't have one, perhaps you'd like to get involved in starting one up. The National Confederation of Parent Teacher Associations has loads of information on its website, which will provide you with all the help and guidance you need.

It's fair to say that you need to bring a certain level of commitment and keenness when you become a member of a PTA – particularly if you take on a role such as chair, secretary or treasurer. You'll be needed to attend as many meetings as possible and you may feel a bit under pressure to take an active role in anything that's being organised, which, over the course of a school year, can add up to quite a number of different things. (One former PTA member admits to being quite peeved when it became clear she was one of just six people left to clear up after a school fête, once the 'part-time volunteers' had gone home!) As well as the satisfaction of knowing that you're doing your bit to help, the bonus of joining is that you're likely to make some good friends and have fun. Many a PTA meeting will start in the school hall and move on to the pub!

Even if you can't join the PTA, there'll be lots of opportunities to help them out on a more ad hoc basis (see page 159). And even if that's not possible, make sure you support all the sterling work they do by turning up to as many of their events as possible – especially the ones that involve fund-raising. Apart from showing you care, you'll get a chance to make yourself known to teachers and other parents, as well as giving your child the opportunity to mix with school mates outside school hours.

Becoming a governor

An even more dedicated role is that of school governor. Governors make up a team of people who work closely with the head teacher to make key decisions about how the school is run. They are also responsible for appointing the head teacher and for overseeing his or her role within the school. They play an important part in improving standards throughout the school, both practically and educationally, and manage the school's budget. Different individuals are given different roles, depending on particular areas of strength, but all governors play a bit part in the smooth running of the school.

If your child attends a school, you can be elected as a parent governor by the parents. The elections are organised by the schools themselves. You can also become a governor either by approaching the school to see if they will co-opt you or by asking your LA, church or foundation if they will appoint you. There may or may not be spaces available on the board and if it's something you're keen to do, you might have to wait.

You can, to an extent, choose the level of involvement you have as a parent governor, although there are certain key meetings you must be available to attend, and these will very often be in the evening. The board of governors must meet at least once a term and you will probably be asked to join at least one committee, which will meet on separate occasions. There may be a lot of paperwork to plough through. But giving your time to the school as a governor usually means you'll get a lot back. It could also stand you in good stead when job-seeking, as you'll have experience of chairing meetings, putting forward suggestions and asking the right questions, public speaking, appointing staff, and helping other members.

There's more information on the websites of GoverNet, the official website for school governors, and the National Governors' Association.

Setting up a parent council

Recent legislation means that, by law, all state schools must take account of parents' views. As part of this, parents are now being encouraged to set up parent-led bodies, usually known as parent councils or forums, in the hope that they will have a positive impact on parents, staff and pupils. Parent councils can't make decisions, as their role is intended to be advisory and consultative, but they should serve an important role in any decision-making process. If there's not one at your school, perhaps you'd like to look into the possibility of setting one up?

There's more information, including advice on how to go about starting a parent council, at the Parent Councils UK website (see page 198).

Parent helper

There'll undoubtedly be opportunities to be a parent helper at school. Expect to feel a real glow if you do give your time (even if washing out paint pots isn't your idea of a great time). Teachers will be in your debt – and many of the children will think you're fantastic, too.

In particular, your support in the classroom may be appreciated. It's a great way to see first-hand how the school and staff operate and to get to know some of the personalities, both adults and kids. It's also lovely for your child to see you playing a part in his school's day (although some schools prefer parents not to be in the same classroom as their own child in case it's a distraction).

Usually you can choose to help as much or as little as you like. It's reasonable for the school to expect a degree of commitment, though, so that they can plan who will be around to help and when: it would be helpful if you can turn up at the same time every week, and if you know you won't be available on a day you would normally help out, for you to give as much notice as possible so other arrangements can be made.

As well as listening to children read individually, you may be asked to help with reading in a group (guided reading), supervising painting and craft work, changing books or maths games, helping with cooking or gardening projects, photocopying and laminating, preparing raw materials and equipment, and tidying up and filing children's work.

Outside of the classroom, there may be a regular role as playtime or lunchtime supervisor, working in the library, or helping in the office. And if you're skilled in any way, perhaps you'll be of particular use, especially when it comes to extra-curricular sessions or clubs – so don't be shy if you can play a musical instrument, cook, sew, garden, play netball, tell stories, or are good at gardening or with computers. Admin skills such as typing or bookkeeping may also be appreciated. Let the school know if you're happy to share and ask if they would welcome your input: even if not straight away, they might want to make a note of your special interest and give you a shout in due course.

If you can't or don't want to make a regular commitment, there'll always be chances to help on an ad hoc basis: making costumes for plays, taking a stand at the summer fête, or coming along as an extra pair of hands on school trips are all roles that need filling from time to time.

Getting CRB checked

Everyone involved in working with children should undergo a Criminal Records Bureau (CRB) check. The CRB is run as an executive agency of the Home Office by civil servants and the service is offered as a way of protecting children from contact with unsuitable people. Everyone working in any capacity at your child's school will have had one, and if you volunteer to help – even if it's just to hear children read or chaperone them on a trip – you'll need to undergo one of these checks. It's a simple, free process that involves filling out a form and providing some forms of identification that will be forwarded to the CRB by the school. It can take several weeks to get clearance from the CRB, after which you will be given a certificate as proof of your check. Having a criminal record won't necessarily preclude you from volunteering within the school, only a conviction that could involve any risk to children.

Emma says: Class teachers are almost always looking for parents to listen to children read or change reading books, so will probably really appreciate any help that you can offer. If you think that your child would be unsettled having you in the classroom, then you can ask to help out in another class. Often schools will put together a list of parents who are willing to help, so it's worth having a chat with the class teacher to see if there is anything that you can assist with. In the first few weeks she may be glad of an extra pair of hands to help the children remove coats and find their pegs, for example. If helping in the classroom is not your thing, then maybe the school would like help with photocopying or organising the library.

Dr Bob says: One way of judging a school's effectiveness is to note how they manage to involve the parents. Some schools put up artificial barriers with an implicit message to parents not to cross them. A really good school will be constantly seeking ways to get parents into the school, both informally and on slightly more formal occasions, to give feedback on their child's progress. If you are going to be a classroom volunteer, psychologically speaking, it's normally better for a parent to help out in a class other than in their child's own. It can be unsettling for a child to have a parent present, and it can make it more difficult for them to differentiate between home and school, parent and teacher. At the same time, it's hard for most parents to give their full attention to the other children when their own child is present.

What the netmums say

Getting involved

I recently became a governor at my son's school, as I've been helping with reading once a week since he started in Reception and, now he's in Year 2, I want to 'give a bit more'. It's early days yet but I am enjoying it very much. I expected the training day to be painful, but in fact it was excellent, relevant and superbly well run. One key thing is that they reminded us we weren't there to bring everyone's moans and groans to the table, but had been elected by the parents to give our views as representatives of the parent body. The mantra should be, 'What difference will this make to the children?' in all that we discuss. From my experience to date, I'd highly recommend it.
Sharon from Fleet, mum to Elliot, six

I made a conscious decision not to join the PTA, as I know people who've done so and found it a hell of a commitment (if rewarding). Instead, I've made myself a reliable volunteer at most events: Christmas fair, summer fête and school discos (fairly terrifying experiences which demand resilience to noise and a willingness to mop up tears!). I also go and help with the Reception class for a few hours on a Friday. I find the chaos and mess quite a challenge – but most of them are so adorable and I know I'm appreciated, so it's worthwhile.
Julia from Milton Keynes, mum to Nina, seven, and Ellie, four

Working full-time means it's hard to get involved at school and I regret that sometimes. But I do my bit where possible: I will always make cakes for fêtes and fairs, and I look out old clothes if they do a collection.
Alison from Littlehampton, mum to Cameron, seven, and Sadie, three

I loved being part of the PTA. I was a member throughout my kids' time at primary school, and chair of it for two years. I was only working part-time hours then and had quite a bit of time to spare, so it was something I was glad to do. The best bit was being in and around school so much, feeling a part of the community there and knowing the teachers thought highly of me. The worst was trying to drum up enthusiasm sometimes among more apathetic parents!
Miriam from Buxton, mum to Scott, eleven, and Stephanie, nine

Supporting your child (without taking over)

Starting school and thriving in a school environment is a big deal for a little one, and support will certainly be needed, especially in the early days. There's a fine line between being a supportive parent and being pushy. But if you can stay on the right side of it, you'll be an invaluable help to your child.

How to be 'all ears'

The key skill required for being supportive – in any situation – is the ability to listen. That might mean sitting down at the end of each school day and chatting things through with your child; or, if you find it easier, talking while you're doing something else like driving or unpacking the weekly shop. Other times, though, it might mean reading between the lines a little, perhaps probing a bit to see if something is going on that your child can't or won't express.

It's important to have regular 'catch-ups' with him, whether or not he seems happy – and even if he's a bit reluctant to go over his day. (It's not at all unusual for primary-age children, who famously 'live in the moment' to claim to have forgotten everything they did during the school day. But don't worry, with a bit of prompting they can usually remember a good deal of it in the end!) Ask him what his favourite part of the day was; what he was less keen on; who he played with; whether there were any problems; and whether he likes his teacher – and if not, why not. If your child seems resistant to the idea of talking with you about his day – whether or not there seems to be something wrong – you could try some of the tips in the box on the next page.

Tricks for talking

- Instigate a chat when you're driving somewhere together: some children prefer to chat when there's no direct eye contact. (It can work when you're having a tricky conversation with an adult, too!)
- Go somewhere other than home, like a tea shop or park, so that the chat can then be left there when you go home again. This can make it seem more casual.
- Chat about your own day, or your own feelings. If you open up first, maybe he'll open up in return.
- If he's reluctant to talk, see if you can encourage a bit of role play: say, for instance, 'I wonder how your teddy would have enjoyed today if he'd been there with you?' and see if 'teddy' has anything he'd like to change or put right.

Dr Bob says: Listening is a much more difficult skill than is often realised – it requires the ability not to interrupt or to chip in with your own interpretation of events. When you are listening to your child, it is also important for you to realise and accept that you cannot make all problems go away or necessarily come up with a ready solution. In my experience, a mother's intuition that something is wrong with their child is rarely wrong. If you feel that something at school isn't quite right, take the matter seriously while trying not to come across as an over-anxious parent.

The importance of being positive

If there's one thing you should be when it comes to supporting your child at school, it's positive. Showing him that you are enthusiastic about and interested in everything he's learning means those attitudes are likely to rub off on him. Again, there's a fine line between positivity and pushiness: try too hard and it's likely to be off-putting. You'll have to work out for yourself where that line lies.

How you respond to and encourage your child will depend to an extent on how he sees himself. Some children will try and try again until they master something; others write themselves off as 'useless' when they fall at the first hurdle. If your child is rather negative about his abilities, try to focus on anything he achieves that shows effort or improvement. So you might say: 'That handwriting is even better than last time you tried' or 'That's right, try it again and it'll probably get easier' or 'Good boy! You've written a few lines already! Now, how about trying just a few more?'

Dr Bob says: The current psychological term for instilling positivity in a child is 'learned optimism', which is in sharp contrast to the opposite approach of 'learned helplessness'. Studies have shown that optimism adds to one's chances of success in all forms of endeavour, while pessimism is more likely to lead to failure.

Emma says: Thinking of new ways to approach a task can help your child feel motivated. If he is learning words, then you could try making them into a board game or sticking them up around the house. If he is struggling with calculations then a trip to the supermarket or a spot of cooking together can help you use the methods in real-life situations. Linking homework to a favourite sport or TV character can help to make it seem more interesting and encourage those children who may be struggling a little. If you have children of different ages, then sitting everyone down at the same time can help to motivate the younger children and creates a quiet house while they work.

Praise where praise is due

Be sure to praise every achievement your child makes, no matter how small. It's well known that children respond much better to praise than to criticism, and your child is more likely to try even harder after you've given him some well-earned words of encouragement, than if you tell him he must try harder in order to succeed. Remember to praise effort, too.

Not all parents find it easy giving out praise – perhaps because they were not themselves praised much as children. If this is the case, you'll need to try to put your own experience behind you and break the cycle.

Don't feel you have to go overboard with praise, and do use it appropriately. Experts advise that you be always specific, so he's in no doubt as to what you're praising him for.

> ***Dr Bob says:*** It's important to remember that inappropriate praise can have a long-term detrimental effect. One psychologist has shown that children who receive nothing but praise can find it difficult to discriminate between those actions that warrant it and those that don't. This is one reason why it's important to describe exactly what it is you're praising when you praise your child.

Rewarding effort and achievement

If you think your child has achieved something worthy of celebrating in a bigger way than praise alone, give him a reward. It needn't be ostentatious, or cost you any money. Perhaps you could cook his favourite supper; tell him he can invite a friend round to play; allow him an extra 15 minutes up before bedtime; promise him a swimming trip at the weekend; or treat him to some new stickers or other small collectable. You may already have a reward system or chart up and running at home.

As with praise, it's a good idea to make sure he knows specifically what you're rewarding him for. Keep rewards in proportion to your child's achievements, and you'll always have something to pull out of the bag for when he does something really impressive!

Learning with you

There's no doubt that much of a child's learning – particularly in the early years – takes place at home as well as at school. You can boost your little one's chances of doing well, and help to compound everything that he's absorbing at school by making sure he learns loads when he's with you, too.

You don't have to sit your child down with paper, pen and books to encourage learning (and, in fact, you shouldn't). At this age, it's all about learning through play – so, as long as you're playing with your child, or encouraging him to play on his own or with friends, then you're helping with his learning. And there are many examples of how his language and number skills can be boosted with your guidance through games, activities and chat: talking about pictures in books, for example; looking for differences and similarities in everyday things; simple board games; pointing out colours, shapes and sizes; repeating nursery rhymes and songs; counting steps or crayons; identifying letters on cereal packets; and naming animals or plants. It's all education!

> ***Dr Bob says:*** Play is generally considered by psychologists to be one of the most important aspects of children's learning development. Sometimes it's important to encourage children to enjoy open-ended, creative play, where they set their own agenda. At other times, it's really helpful to provide

structured play activities that help to develop the skills he needs for academic learning. Old favourites, like board games, help to develop counting and turn-taking skills, while jigsaw puzzles need attention, concentration and logic as well as developing spatial skills. There is an enormous range of games which will help to reinforce many developmental skills and thinking strategies.

The more serious stuff!

Sooner or later, his learning will also involve more serious stuff like reading, writing and number work. You can help with that, too, and the school will generally be glad for you to do so: they've probably got some useful handouts with practical advice on how best you can do it and it's a good idea to take careful note to ensure you're using the same strategies for learning that his teacher is. If you're using the methods you learned at school, chances are you're out of date. Modern strategies in primary schools include the use of phonics for reading, where children learn to recognise the sounds of parts of words before putting them together and eventually recognising whole words, and number bonds in maths, where children learn all the different calculations that will arrive at a given number, for example, that by adding 1 to 6, 2 to 5 or 3 to 4 they will arrive at 7. Of course, teaching methods vary, so don't guess, find out specifically how your child's teachers work.

Bear in mind, too, that it's vital to take this stuff at your child's pace – pushing him to make achievements could really put him off.

If it turns out your child is brighter than average, you might want to give him a few extra challenges in addition to his schoolwork, to avoid him becoming bored. Don't make assumptions, though: ask his teachers if and how you can help. If he's genuinely gifted, they'll pick it up and, just as they would do for children whose learning isn't progressing so well, they'll adapt the curriculum to his needs and, if appropriate, place him on their Gifted and Talented Register. All schools must keep this list of pupils who would benefit from being stretched, and provide extra challenges and activities for them.

Emma says: Most teachers will be more than happy to explain all the different methods that are used in school. They understand that it can be confusing when your child is using modern methods that you didn't use. It can be very helpful because it will mean that you feel more confident about helping your child at home. The class teacher will also be happy to explain the routines of the classroom and the behaviour expectations that may need reinforcing at home. A good starting point is to ask for a copy of the termly plan. This will allow you to see which topics your child will be covering and will help you to plan activities that support their learning. If they are, for example, learning about castles at school, then a family trip to a local castle could really develop their interest and enhance their understanding; or if they are exploring toys at school, then perhaps you could dig out some of your old toys for them to look at and compare with their own.

Dr Bob says: It's important that parents try not to live through their children, unconsciously using them to achieve their own thwarted ambitions. One of the most difficult tasks any parent has is to encourage and facilitate children to develop at their own pace in areas they're naturally drawn to, rather than being pushed. As a psychologist I have never met a parent who didn't want what was best for their child, but sometimes a parent's views about how to achieve the best can be at odds with the child's real needs.

Helping with homework

Different schools have different policies on homework, with some more hardline than others. But, in most, there should be little or none during Reception and what you *do* get shouldn't be a chore. You may be asked to do a little reading, learning of key words, or perhaps a weekly maths- or literacy-based game. Or it might involve a fun task that isn't really 'work' at all, such as looking out a photograph, or coming back with the answer to a simple question.

While helping with any amount of homework is a task most parents could do without and, after a hard day's graft at school, it doesn't really seem fair that children have do it, either, it's a fact of school life. As the amount and importance of it will increase over the years, it's a good idea to get into good habits early: so make sure your child completes what's been asked of him, give him whatever help he needs, and remain upbeat and consistent about it.

When there's a task to be done, aim to do it after he's had a rest, but before it gets close to bedtime, when he'll be tired. Listening to your little one read is particularly important, so do get in whatever reading practice you can manage. Make sure he's comfortable, fed and watered, and that there's no noise or distraction. Never force it, though, or make your little one read if he's tired – it will be counterproductive.

> ***Emma says:*** If your child has a particular interest, then try to incorporate this into their homework. A football-themed board game might motivate them to learn spellings more than a simple list of words. If your child finds it hard to sit down and concentrate, how about throwing beanbags into hoops that are labelled with the different words that they are learning to read, or jumping on cut-outs of initial letters as you read out the words.

What the Netmums say

Supporting children (without pushing)

Ryan really struggled with pencil control at first, so I bought him a set of cool dinosaur stencils, which he was very keen to use. They only really work if you use a pencil or felt pen, not crayons, which he was more used to, so it made him try harder to get the control. I used to hold the top of the pencil gently so I could help him guide it, but it wasn't long before he got really confident. Now he has no problems.
Maura from Newport, mum to Ryan, five

Dan wasn't doing so well at first with reading or writing, but his hand-eye co-ordination has always been good so he was great at sports, games and model-making. Luckily his teacher spotted his potential in these areas and has given him all due encouragement. He's a child who doesn't respond very well to pressure, so praising him on what he was good at and down-playing his academic progress was just what he needed in Reception. Now, in Year 2, he's starting to catch up and I don't feel very worried. His self-esteem is pretty high as he's football captain for his year.
Kathy from Wolverhampton, mum to Daniel, six

Archie is young for his year and wanted to do lots of playing after school, so sometimes getting him to do homework could be difficult. We got homework on Mondays and it had to be done by the following Friday (apart from reading) so I would plan with him when he was going to do it and when he was going to play, and he was fine with that. Fortunately he loved reading so he wanted to do that every night.
Lucy from Dunblane, mum to Archie, six, and Dugald, four

We feel that the best thing we can do for our daughter, who attends a special school, is to follow up approaches and strategies carried out with her in school at home, and to involve other people who have contact with her, particularly grandparents, so as to ensure a consistent approach to supporting her learning. We want to reinforce learning methods and ways of encouraging desired behaviour so that she develops and improves on problem areas.
Nicola from Redcar, mum to Natasha, five

Tilly used to love her bath books and board books as a baby, but as soon as she had to do reading every day for school she stopped wanting to read anything else. She's always been a bit resistant to people telling her what to do, so I think it was her way of rebelling a little bit. I was quite upset as I'm a great reader myself and I wanted her to enjoy reading for pleasure, but the signs were that she'd been turned right off. I decided not to push in any way, and let her become interested in her own time. I needn't have worried – she's reading again now, probably because she's so much better at it and she can get through the pages quite quickly.
Barbara from Halifax, mum to Tilly, seven

We tend to reward our daughter after parents' nights with a trip to the fish and chip shop – although I'm not sure if it's more of a reward for her or for us! I also make a point of making a big deal out of good behaviour as well as academic achievement, as they can't all be top of the class.
Gail from Peterborough, mum to Katie, five, and Jack, two

Class struggles

It may be that your little one turns out to struggle with some aspects of his learning during his first year at school. It's worth remembering that children can take a whole year to settle in to the business of learning, particularly if they're among the younger ones in the class. If this is the case, you may not even get to hear about it and it's perfectly likely you won't have to be worried. Or the teacher may discuss it with you but tell you that they are not concerned at this point. A little extra support from staff at school will be all that's required.

If you are told – either during his first year, or beyond – that your child needs some 'extra help', don't panic. It doesn't necessarily mean he has a recognised learning difficulty or a special educational need: it may simply mean that he needs a bit more time and attention to fulfill his potential. It could be that his teacher has to adjust the requirements of the National Curriculum slightly (known as 'differentiating'), or teach in a slightly different way to suit his needs. Or they may arrange for him to have some extra help with a classroom or learning support assistant, individually or in a group, or provide some specialist equipment, such as a computer. And 'extra help' will most likely be a short-term measure, so if it's something your child is offered, think of it as a positive move forward. And just because he needs some at one point, it doesn't mean he'll need it throughout his entire time at school.

Emma says: Certainly, some difficulties with learning can be linked to a child's age or issues with settling in. Summer-born children who have joined the school in September, for example, can appear to be struggling a little, but with additional support they make good progress. Parents should remember that learning does not follow a simple upwards curve – it has ups, downs and can plateau from time to time. Schools will be very experienced at picking up any issues and ensuring that extra support is put in place if it is needed.

Special educational needs

When a more significant learning difficulty is identified, a child is said to have special educational needs (SEN). It may be that, if your child has SEN, they've already been identified (if not formally diagnosed) while in a pre-school setting. Or it may be that it's something that isn't picked up until he's in school. It's natural to feel a bit alarmed if the phrase 'special educational needs' is mentioned. But the first thing to bear in mind is that it refers to a wide spectrum of issues and won't necessarily mean a more serious disorder such as dyspraxia, autism or Attention Deficit Hyperactivity Disorder (ADHD). The second is that, if it *has* been picked up and your child's school is telling you they plan to help, then that's a positive thing indeed.

Once a special need has been identified, the child's parent, their teacher and the school's special education needs co-ordinator (SENCO) will meet to discuss what his needs are and how he's going to get them. Usually, an individual education plan (IEP) will be drawn up, setting out a series of targets and how he can be helped to meet them. This sort of support is part of a process called School Action. If, after a while, it seems obvious that help is still needed, the school may arrange for someone from outside school to come in and assess the situation, for example, an educational psychologist (EP) or a speech and language therapist. This is known as School Action Plus.

Occasionally, if their needs are serious enough, a parent, or the school, or the combined forces of both, can ask the local education authority to assess them for a Statement of Educational Needs – a legally enforceable document setting out his precise needs and the financial provision that will be made for them. If they agree to an assessment, the 'statementing' process that follows can be long, complicated and bureaucratic, and a significant number of applications are unsuccessful.

How you can help

Whatever the reason or the extent of your little one's class struggles, he'll need plenty of extra help and support, emotionally and practically, from you. All the ideas for learning at home outlined above will become even more important. And giving him even more reassurance, praise and encouragement will matter, too.

Good communication with school – both ways – will also be a must. Listen carefully to anything you're being told by the experts, but equally make sure that any concerns you have are being acknowledged. Get advice and information from outside school to help you. Good sources include the Advisory Centre for Education (ACE) and the Independent Panel for Special Educational Advice (IPSEA). You could also contact your local Parent Partnership Association, an organisation that provides impartial advice and information to parents of children with special educational needs.

Emma says: It can be a difficult time for children and their parents when special education needs are first noticed. But schools will have lots of experience of these early days and a wealth of specialist knowledge to draw upon. If a child in Reception is placed on an IEP, it's often a short-term step to tackle a specific issue – it does not mean that they will have SEN throughout their school career. For some children the support will be ongoing and, as a parent, you should be fully involved in the plans that are put in place to support your child. A SENCO may become involved if the Reception teacher flags up concerns and will be involved from the start if a child is entering the school with recognised SEN.

Dr Bob says: If you and your child's teacher do suspect that your child has special or additional needs, it's quite likely that the school will recommend you have a chat with their visiting educational psychologist, who may also be asked to carry out some form of assessment of your child's strengths and weaknesses. This is not a psychiatrist (who provides help for adults and/or children with emotional difficulties), but an educational expert with a psychology degree and knowledge about child development. Unfortunately, there are still too few educational psychologists available on a regular basis for most schools, so you may have to wait some time for an appointment.

Supporting friendships

Your child may forge and lose friendships frequently during his early years at school, and this is quite normal while he's finding his feet and working out the types of children whose company he most enjoys. Expect lots of declarations of 'best' friendships, followed by sudden cooling-off periods and complete changes of allegiance – all are very common at this early age and it often isn't until junior school that really strong bonds are formed.

For this reason, it's usually no cause for a great deal of concern if he seems to be spending a lot of time with friends you may not necessarily have picked for him. These different friendships will play different roles in their formative years: the more boisterous child might bring a shyer individual out of his shell, or send him running for cover; quiet, withdrawn children can either provoke sympathy in others who will naturally try to draw him into their group, or may become the subject of teasing; and very bright children can be the envy of others, or may be considered geeky. Forming relationships with different sorts of children is a good experience for life, so go along with all of his (unless bullying becomes an issue – see page 182).

Your best strategy – whatever your child's personality – is to make regular offers to have other children home for tea or weekend visits. Let your child choose who he would like to ask, but don't leave it up to him to make any arrangements – find the relevant parents in the playground or give your child a note to send home to his friend's mum, then take things from there. Bear in mind that the other parent may want to accompany their child unless they already know you: imagine how you would feel sending your child to an unknown person's house for the first time.

You don't have to supervise your child's every moment with a playmate, but do make sure you've got plenty of things planned for them to play with or do, especially if either of them seems to feel a bit awkward at first. A puzzle can be a good ice-breaker, as can a popular DVD – and if you sit them in front of a film at first, chances are they'll soon make their way off to play upstairs. If you have a garden and the weather is fine, set out some play equipment and leave them to it.

Emma says: If you're worried that your child is struggling to make friends then the class teacher should be able to reassure you. It is possible that he or she plays with lots of the children, but hasn't settled on one person as a best friend. There are many ways that the teacher can help to encourage friendships. Often schools will have a 'buddy system' operating in the playground so that children are not alone. The older children may be encouraged to set up group games and ask the younger children to join in.

Inviting another child home for a play date can be a really good way of helping your child create friendships and it gives you the chance to see how your child plays. If your child is particularly shy, then you might like to have a couple of activities planned, like making pizzas together or junk modelling. Hopefully your child will receive a return invite and you'll get the chance to get to know other mums.

You are invited to . . . .

When your child starts school, so does the social whirl! As a rule, expect lots of party invites in the first year (and the second, too, although they start to tail off after that and begin to give way to more exclusive events, special outings and even sleepovers).

It's not unusual for parties during the first year or two of school to involve the whole class: probably because, at this stage, most parents don't know exactly who their child has chummed up with and partly because it can feel so unfair inviting some and not others. And, of course, once one child has a big party, other parents come under pressure to do the same. Then you end up worrying about returning invites for any your child has previously received!

If a party that large seems like a practical or financial impossibility, one solution is to team up with another parent with a child whose birthday is around the same time – that way, you can split costs and organisational duties. (You can ask guests to bring just one suitable present, rather than two, then split the pile in half, which reduces the cost for them and means your child doesn't have a rather excessive pile of 30 presents to work his way through after the party.)

If you can only face or afford a smaller gathering, you'll have to ask your child to pick a limited number of friends from his class. (This can have pitfalls, though, as he may not be sure who his friends are; he may leave some off the list by mistake; and he may lose or acquire some in the period between issuing invites and the party!)

Issuing invitations can be awkward if you're inviting some children and not others – you might have to be sensitive about where and when you hand them out (and it's better if *you* do this job – if you ask your child to, there's a good chance some or all of them won't reach the intended recipients, or they will but the intended recipient won't then hand it on to *his* mum!). Sometimes teachers or classroom assistants are happy to help when it comes to giving out party invites, and may even be willing to put them in bags for you or hand them out at the end of the school day: but it's likely they'll only want to do this if the whole class is involved, to avoid hurt feelings. (In fact, some schools actually request that you don't issue party invites in or around school at all for this reason.)

When friendships go wrong

We adults all know that the course of friendship doesn't always run smooth – and the same is equally true for kids of all ages. The difference is it doesn't take much to spoil or end a friendship when you're four or five. Sometimes a disagreement about who supports which football team or whose lunchbox is the best will be the final straw in an otherwise harmonious relationship! Girls can be more prone to break-ups than boys – for unknown and no doubt complex psychological reasons – but, in any case, young children can take disputes very much to heart, so it's important to take their disappointment (if not the trigger for it) seriously.

If your child comes home from school obviously upset about a falling out with a friend, sit down with him, give him a cuddle and gently encourage him to talk about it. It's easier to coax feelings out if you can reassure him that you understand and acknowledge what he is feeling. So you might say, for example, 'I remember how it felt when I fell out with my best friend when I was your age – it really made me feel sad. I was worried whether I'd be able to find another friend or just be left out of everything. Are you worrying like I was?' Don't try to jolly him straight out of it, or tell him to pull himself together. He'll end up feeling he has no one on his side.

If you suspect he might be the cause of the upset himself (and, hard as it can be to be unbiased sometimes, you need to consider this as a possibility) you could go a bit further with your chat. So you might say, 'I wonder how your friend is feeling. Do you think he's upset, too?' You could perhaps offer to go along with him to make the reconciliation. While it's important to be sympathetic, however, don't make heavy weather of these little hiccups in relationships – and don't be tempted to plough in and sort things out unless the problem seems serious. In most cases, friends can, and will, resolve differences entirely without adult input. If the dispute seems unable to be fixed, you can encourage other friendships by inviting some different children home to play.

Dr Bob says: It's probably true to say that friendships constitute one of the most significant features of a child's school career. In a research project designed to identify what mattered most to children moving from primary to secondary school, a colleague and I discovered that making new friends was seen as even more important than any academic feature.

What the netmums say

Supporting friendships

I was quite reluctant to set up play dates at first because Daniel's group of friends used to change almost daily, but in the end it helped to cement some friendships. I'd ask three friends at a time so that it wasn't too one-to-one at first, then see which of those children he got on with best and asked them around on their own the next time. I think in Daniel's case there were just too many children around him at school for him to make proper friends, and giving him more concentrated time in smaller groups really helped.
Jenni from Blackburn, mum to Daniel, five

Jamie has made several close friends, which I'm pleased about. He's already been on a play date with one little boy in his class and it was a good chance to get friendly with the other mum as I was also invited. I'm planning to return the favour soon.
Ruth from Lancaster, mum to Jamie, four

Lois was so excited going back to school after Christmas, she couldn't wait to see all her little friends again. I'm a working mum so it's difficult to have pals over for tea, but we do have meet-ups during the holidays, and we have had girly evenings shopping or bowling with her friends and their mums.
Jacqui from Gravesend, mum to Lois, six

If ever Lucy is left out of games I tell her that there will always be someone to play with as long as she's being nice, and when certain little groups won't let her play I've told her to take a look around the playground until she spots another lonely face and then go and say hello. She's so pleased with herself when she comes out telling me, 'So-and-so wouldn't let me play so I found a little girl who looked sad and I taught her how to skip!'

Lee from Doncaster, mum to Abi, seven, Lucy, five, and Evie, two

Bullying

Although pretty unusual at this tender age, bullying can sometimes occur within Reception classes. As a rule, teachers will be right on top of it if they notice it. But if you have concerns that it's happening but not being picked up, arrange to talk to your child's teacher about it. Anti-bullying policies are in place in all schools and so, in theory, it's an issue that should be sorted straight away.

If you find out *your* child has been guilty of bullying behaviour, don't overeact: most children are involved in being unkind to another child at some point while at school. Make sure he knows the behaviour is totally unacceptable, but don't label him a bully or reject him. Try to get him to see things from the bullied child's point of view and get him to imagine how he or she feels. And remain positive: look for any good behaviour he shows around the same time and praise it, even if it's something small.

Dr Bob says: One sign of a really good school is where they have a 'buddy' system. Essentially this involves older children being given the responsibility for looking after a younger child on entry to school. The 'buddy' makes sure that the new entrant can find their way around and feels safe in the playground, making sure that they have someone to turn to immediately if they are upset. Some schools even have a 'bus stop' or special bench in the playground that any child can go and stand under, or sit on, if they feel miserable or upset. An older child will then take responsibility for ensuring that they have someone to play with or to sort out their problems. In such schools bullying is invariably absent or at a minimum.

Helping your child to accept differences

Schools are great melting pots: if he hasn't yet been exposed to people and other children who are a bit different in some way, your child soon will be. It's more than likely there'll be kids of different colours, shapes, abilities and family situations for him to get to meet and know.

Fortunately children are pretty open minded by nature – although they can be cruel if they come up against something they don't understand – and most schools should be doing a good job of integrating all children and encouraging friendships among the whole group (as part of the EYFS theme of positive relationships, which includes respecting each other). There are also lots of different sorts of people on our television screens these days, which is all for the good. You can do your bit at home, too, by talking the issues through. Of course, the best thing you can do is set the right example – so make sure he always sees that you accept people are different, too.

Getting on with other parents

It's true that other parents can be one of the challenges of school life. But they can also be one of the bonuses – many, many good friendships and some truly great ones have been forged as a result of people meeting through school. And a million cracking mums' nights out have been organised on the back of the school run.

School gate politics can, unfortunately, cause unpleasantness sometimes, though, affecting other parents you know, if not you directly. 'Cliquishness', in particular, can lead to hurt feelings. (One mum who offered her services at the summer fête turned up hours before the start only to be shunned by all the stallholders and consigned to running a 'lob the wet sponge' stall on her own with no one to relieve her.) Avoid getting drawn in if this happens: sidestep any nastiness by claiming ignorance and changing the subject. If it's tempting (and even, frankly, enjoyable) to join in with gossip about a certain parent or child, try to imagine how you'd feel if it were you.

Fortunately, school gate experiences are mostly harmless and very often good. When you start as a new parent, the few minutes before and after school – and any other occasions when you come face to face with other parents – offer a great chance to meet mums in the same boat. And, with such a big thing in common, you will always, always have something to talk about, which is good news for shy people.

If you're someone who has no problem talking to new people and meeting new friends, or if you've got to the point where your place outside the school gates is well established, spare a thought for the newer or shyer ones. A mum who keeps herself to herself may be crying out for someone friendly to make the first move. Be sure to be generous with your smiles and hellos, and maybe start a conversation, too.

And don't forget dads! Blokes are more and more frequent fixtures at the school gates these days, thanks to the increasing take-up of flexible hours and broadening social attitudes. You might even find the ratio of mums and dads doing the school run is close to 50–50 at your school. But whether dads are a minority or not, don't ignore them. Try to involve them in your conversations: and consider the fact that *they* might appreciate an invite to that coffee morning as much as the next parent.

Of course, a few parents simply aren't interested in integrating – perhaps they have quite enough friends of their own already. (Maybe you even feel this way yourself.) Respect this, if you believe it's the case. Exchange pleasantries, but don't get in their faces.

Just like your child's friendships, parents' friendships can ebb and flow (often simultaneously) during the primary school years; and if there are times when they go a bit wrong, well, the playground's a busy place, and it's usually easy enough to avoid someone for a little while. Don't be childish about it, though. Make friends again as soon as possible – if you're going to be passing every day, twice a day, for the next four and a half years, being on bad terms could become pretty awkward.

If you're keen to make friends and you're not sure how, get involved in any social events put on at the school. Lots of parents sort things out for themselves, too. If someone hasn't suggested a big night out for the mums in your child's class before the first term is up, then do so yourself. You don't have to do anything expensive – just arrange to meet in a local pub. Or you could suggest a bring-a-dish night, if someone with a large-ish house or garden is prepared to host – every person brings one item of food, with a fair-sized buffet the result.

Avoiding competitive parent syndrome

Of course you're proud of your little one. Every parent is. But there are few things more irritating than competitive parents, so try to keep your pride in check outside school – you can bang on about how wonderful he is later, to your other half or to his grandparents (who, of course, will entirely agree).

If and when you come up against parents who are unable to stop showing off when it comes to their offspring's achievements or aptitude (and you will), humour them. They may well want you to know that their child is up to white level in reading, or they got the most prizes under their belt during sports day, but grit your teeth and smile. Resist the temptation to one-up them by reeling off your own child's plus points, and if you have to concede that their kid's achievements really are more impressive than yours, do so to yourself, quietly. Don't let your own child know that you're anything other than proud of him!

What the netmums say

Getting on with other parents

The playground has proved to be a great place to meet fellow mums who I can share my doubts, fears and insecurities with: it can really help just knowing there is someone else in the same boat!
Ruth from Lancaster, mum to Jamie, four

We don't have contact with any other parents due to the fact that our daughter gets a school bus and the only other adult we speak to is her bus escort. (She attends a special school.) I'm sure that we would find other parents and families approachable should we get the opportunity to meet them. I would have perhaps felt more isolated had I been part of a mainstream school community, as other parents would lack understanding and awareness of our situation and may label our child as a result.
Nicola from Redcar, mum to Natasha, five

I'm quite friendly with a lot of the mums at the school gates. Our children are friends and a lot of them live nearby so we all walk home together. I wouldn't say I've made new friends yet – just 'so-and-so's mum' but then they've only been there six months. I think it will come with time. There are a few competitive parents at the gates. I just keep myself to myself, am friendly with everyone and realise that I don't know what

goes on behind their doors and they don't know what goes on behind mine, and we'll probably never know or understand each other's lives.
Aimee from Chester, mum to Lauren and Megan, five, and Sophie, three

I was a bit dismayed when I tried to break in to a few cliques in the playground and was given the cold shoulder. Lots of the parents already had kids further up the school so knew each other well and weren't particularly welcoming. Before long I made a couple of friends among other mums who had just one child at the school, though, and I'm going to make a conscious effort to welcome the new mums if I have any more children.
Helen from Harrow, mum to Natasha, five

There is a mother of one of the children in my son's class and she takes every opportunity to make the rest of us feel bad. My son was getting upset about it until I explained that we all have strengths in different areas. I have to admit, though, that when she was boasting about her son being very good at swimming and he'd just completed level one, I did have to say, 'Oh really? Jack's just starting level four.' Which he is!
Emma from Enfield, mum to Jack, five

I think that I get along with the other parents. I don't believe in cliques as I was always on the outside when I was at school so I make an effort to speak to everybody. There is a clique but I think that I am lucky to have a foot in all camps.
Clare from Lincoln, mum to Scarlett, five

I absolutely love the fact that I've made so many friends through school, and dozens more acquaintances. Seeing so many friendly faces and saying 'morning' to every other parent just makes the start of my day wonderful. And, of course, there are always loads of people you can turn to if you need a piece of information or some advice about a certain aspect of school life (which I frequently do!). I also enjoy our mums' nights out immensely – all organised while we're waiting for the bell to go.
Julia from Milton Keynes, mum to Nina, seven, and Ellie, four

I think I am the competitive parent! I try hard not to be, but because Toby is brighter than average and tends to have tantrums, which makes it hard for him to make friends, I sometimes can't resist because it helps to be able to 'justify' my son's rather challenging behaviour. Painful, I know! I think if you have sociable, confident children then starting school is an exciting time. For those of us with anxious or challenging children, it can be exhausting and very stressful for the whole family.
Jo from Brackley, mum to Toby, five

The best days of their lives

Don't forget to preserve as many of those precious memories as possible – start up a scrapbook, photo album or file and be sure to put away whatever you can't fit on the fridge or pin board in the way of photographs, certificates, reports, and examples of their art and other work (you'll end up with absolutely masses: some mums are able to bin some of this to keep the paper mountain down, others can't bear to throw away a single finger painting – chances are it will depend on how much storage space you have!). Make sure you've got a school portrait for every year (these can get pretty expensive, but there's usually the option of a single print) and a class line-up, too (don't forget to write down everyone's name, as some are sure to be lost in the mists of time). You might want to put everything into a memory box or make a collage which you can put in a frame on your child's bedroom wall.

Above all, cherish the memories in your mind. Your child's schooldays should be among the best of his life – and pretty good ones for you, too.

Appendix I: What to ask/look for when you are choosing your pre-school setting

- Is there plenty of outdoor space for the children to play in?
- Is the indoor space safe and clean?
- Do the children seem happy and relaxed?
- Is there somewhere for the children to sleep or rest?
- What is the daily routine?
- How will you be kept informed about your child's progress?
- What happens if your child is unhappy? How would she be looked after?
- What are the policies on discipline? How do they manage behaviour?
- What happens if your child is sick? How will they contact you in an emergency?
- Will dietary requirements or allergies be accommodated?
- What is the ratio of staff to children?
- Do they operate a key worker system (i.e. will there be one member of staff with special responsibility for looking after your little one and liaising with you)?

- Do they offer a settling-in period? And, if so, how long is it?
- Will you have to pay for holidays/meals/anything else?
- What's the staff turnover like? How well qualified are the staff? Are all the criminal records checks (see page 160) up to date?
- What Ofsted rating do they have and when is the next inspection due?
- Can you see registration certificates and inspection reports?

Appendix II: What to ask/look for on a school visit

- What is the usual daily routine?
- What arrangements does the school offer for settling your child ahead of joining?
- Is there a breakfast/after-school club? If so, can I meet the staff, and what are their qualifications? What is the ratio of staff to children in the breakfast/after-school club? What are the fees?
- What is the school's behaviour policy?
- How much time is expected to be spent on homework? What sort of input can I give with homework?
- Do you have any printed information on how you teach reading and numbers?
- How do staff handle illness/accidents? (e.g. Can children be picked up and cuddled if they are distressed?)
- Are the classes made up of mixed ages and abilities? Are the classes mixed up each year or not?
- How do you encourage children who find it hard to make friends?
- What is the procedure if I have any concerns about my child?

- How often are the children assessed academically, and how often are the results reported to the parents?
- Are there any planned school trips and, if so, where to?
- What extra learning/teaching resources does the school have?
- Is there work displayed on the walls?
- Are there any reward schemes in evidence?
- If the visit takes place during school time, do the children look happy and engaged?
- What are the resources like?
- Is all equipment up to date and well kept?
- Does the school and its staff offer a welcoming feeling?
- Is it busy and noisy, or smaller and more focused?
- What are the class sizes?
- Is there enough emphasis on play and sporting achievement?
- Do the teachers seem to know each child individually?
- What are school dinners like? How well does the menu cater for special dietary needs?

Appendix III: Sources of help and further information

Early learning and childcare

4Children (national charity aimed at boosting kids' opportunities, with a particular interest in care and early learning): helpline 020 7512 2100; www.4children.org.uk

Daycare Trust: information line 0845 872 6251; www.daycaretrust.org.uk

Early Years (childcare information for Northern Ireland): 028 9066 2825; www.early-years.org

Family Information Service: 0800 2346 346; www.familyinformationservices.org.uk

National Childminding Association: 0845 880 0044; www.ncma.org.uk

National Day Nurseries Association: www.ndna.org.uk

Pre-school Learning Alliance: 020 7833 0991; www.pre-school.org.uk

Scottish Childcare (free impartial information on childcare and early learning across Scotland): www.scottishchildcare.gov.uk

Scottish Pre-school Play Association: 0141 221 4148; www.sppa.org.uk

Wales Pre-school Playgroups Association: 01686 624573; www.walesppa.org

www.childcare.co.uk (independent database of childcare across the UK)

www.daynurseries.co.uk (independent database of day nurseries across the UK)

www.outofschoolalliance.co.uk (practical help and support for out-of-school clubs)

www.underfives.co.uk (lots of general early learning information)

Education and early learning inspectorates

Care and Social Services Inspectorate Wales: www.csiw.wales.gov.uk

Department of Education Northern Ireland: www.deni.gov.uk

Estyn: www.estyn.gov.uk

Her Majesty's Inspectorate of Education (Scotland): www.hmie.gov.uk

Ofsted: helpline 0845 640 4040; www.ofsted.gov.uk

Scottish Commission for the Regulation of Care: www.carecommission.com

General sources of information on education

Advisory Centre for Education (ACE): advice line 0808 800 5793; www.ace-ed.org.uk

British Association for Early Childhood Education: www.early-education.org.uk

Department for Education: www.education.gov.uk

Parentzone (information about education of children from 3 to 18 for Scotland): www.ltscotland.org.uk/parentzone

www.schoolsfinder.direct.gov.uk (schoolfinder page of Direct Gov)

Curriculum and testing

Qualifications and Curriculum Development Agency: www.qcda.gov.uk
SATS (independent website offering information and advice):
www.satsguide.co.uk
School and College Attainment Tables:
www.dcsf.gov.uk/performancetables

Independent schools and home education

Education Otherwise: www.education-otherwise.org
Home Education UK: www.home-education.org.uk
The Independent Schools Council: www.isc.co.uk
The Independent Schools Directory: www.indschools.co.uk
Montessori Society: www.montessori-uk.org
Rudolph Steiner Schools: www.steinerwaldorf.org

Special Educational Needs

British Dyslexia Association (BDA): helpline 0845 251 9002;
www.bdadyslexia.org.uk
Independent Parental Special Education Advice: 0800 018 4016;
www.ipsea.org.uk
National Association for Gifted Children: helpline 0845 450 0295;
www.nagcbritain.org.uk
National Association for Special Educational Needs: www.nasen.org.uk
National Parent Partnership Network: www.parentpartnership.org.uk

Campaigning groups

Parents Aloud (independent organisation with the aim of making
parents' views on education heard): www.parentsoutloud.com
Water is Cool in School: www.wateriscoolinschool.org.uk

School food

School Food Trust: information line 0800 089 5001; www.schoolfoodtrust.org.uk

Soil Association's *Food for Life*: enquiry line 0117 314 5180; www.foodforlife.org.uk

Support for working parents

ACAS: helpline 08457 47 47 47; www.acas.org.uk

Citizens' Advice Bureau: www.adviceguide.org.uk

Family Friendly Working: www.familyfriendlyworking.co.uk

Inland Revenue: tax credits helpline 0845 300 3900; www.hmrc.gov.uk

Working Families: helpline 0800 013 0313; www.workingfamilies.org.uk

Working Mums: www.workingmums.co.uk

www.payingforchildcare.org.uk (part of the Daycare Trust)

Parental input in schools

National Confederation of Parent Teacher Associations: www.ncpta.org.uk

National Governors' Association: www.nga.org.uk

Parent Councils UK: www.parentcouncils.co.uk

www.governornet.co.uk

Bullying

Kidscape (national anti-bullying charity): helpline 08451 205 204; www.kidscape.org.uk

Index

More netmums *titles from Headline*

FEEDING KIDS

with Judith Wills

Every mum faces a daily challenge to make sure her children eat plenty of the right foods. But with our busy lives and junk-food culture, just how do you ensure your tiny terrors get healthy meals every day? How do you make their meals nutritious but delicious without spending hours in the kitchen?

netmums the fastest-growing online parenting organisation in the UK, has joined forces with top nutrition expert Judith Wills to solve all your dinnertime dilemmas. All the recipes come from netmums members and all have been tried and tested.

Easy to prepare and cook, they'll fit perfectly into your busy family life. A wonderful combination of healthy food and food your family will actually enjoy, they made the children who road-tested them so happy they not only cleared their plates, they asked for more!

'netmums has grown into a national institution'

Daily Telegraph

'netmums is the new Mothers' Union' *Sunday Times*

FREE P&P AND UK DELIVERY
(Overseas and Ireland £3.50 per book)

To order, simply call 01235 400 414
visit our website: www.headline.co.uk
or email orders@bookpoint.co.uk

Prices and availability are subject to change without notice.

NON-FICTION/COOKERY 978 0 7553 1605 2

More netmums *titles from Headline*

HOW TO BE A HAPPY MUM

with Siobhan Freegard

Stop trying to be the perfect mum. Learn how to be a happy mum.

Having young children is supposed to be the happiest time of your life. But it's not always easy to make the most of the joys of motherhood. You're tired. The kids are playing up. The fridge is empty. The house is a state. And you can't remember when you last had some time to yourself. But while there's no shortage of advice on how to care for babies and children, who is looking after you?

How to Be a Happy Mum identifies the top ten stresses mothers have to cope with and offers sound advice on how to overcome them – from feelings of loneliness, to quieting tantruming toddlers, to managing a hectic home. The advice comes from hand-selected experts and, most importantly, from other mothers who have been there, done it and lived to tell the tale: the members of netmums the UK's fastest-growing online parenting community.

How to Be a Happy Mum tells you how to care for yourself – the person most likely to be forgotten when raising a family. After all, how can you hope to raise happy children if you haven't discovered how to be a happy mum?

FREE P&P AND UK DELIVERY
(Overseas and Ireland £3.50 per book)

To order, simply call 01235 400 414
visit our website: www.headline.co.uk
or email orders@bookpoint.co.uk

Prices and availability are subject to change without notice.

NON-FICTION/PARENTING 978 0 7553 1606 9